More Than a
Great Wedding
2

Don•Q•Dox

More Than a Great Wedding 2
Creating Healthy Communities
Where Relationships Thrive

Second Edition; completely updated and revised.

© 2015 by Daryl L. Smith
Offered by Don•Q•Dox (www.DonQDox.com)

Design and layout: Carolyn B. Smith

ISBN: 978-0692535714

More Than a Great Wedding 2

CONTENTS

Don•Q•Dox: a resource-creation label of The Orlando Fellowship—
an incarnational, missional-ministry community.

Don•Q—The fictional knight *Don Quixote* (Miguel de Cervantes, 1605),
whose most famous adventure includes meeting the tavern prosti-
tute Aldonza and calling her to become the beautiful Dulcinea.

•Dox—Documents/tools/vehicles for discovery.

As the name implies, we are on a quest to discover life as it was meant to be
and invite others to join that quest. We believe that God's image is planted
deeply within each of us, but most times we cannot hear the call of the "im-
possible dream" without the company of others who can see in us things we
don't see in ourselves.

For

Carolyn—
my life partner for now more than 42 years,
who has helped mold me closer
to what a "partnership" husband should look like
as we've ventured together to discover
God's plan for marriage, family,
and grandparenting;

Dawn Élise (and husband **Blair**),
Andrew Benjamin (and wife **Emily T.**),
Emily Margaret (and husband **Jesse**)—
our amazing children who've watched as we've tried
to create a Creation-model home—
now as it's their turn
we pray that they create their own versions—
better than their parents'
and more like the Original Model;

**Ailey Kaelyn, Etta Gracyn, Benen Andrew, Aryn Élise,
Mikah Marie, and Trae Allen**—
our grandchildren—
wonderful, growing people,
who've quickly worked their way into our hearts, and
whom we pray will always know
Jesus' love deeply
and every relationship
healthy.

With Gratitude...

We never can thank all those who have impacted our lives—shared their wisdom, pushed us to grow, mentored us along the way. Here's a partial list of those who at least need a shout-out for their contribution to this second edition project.

Asbury Theological Seminary—Florida Dunnam Campus faculty/ staff team—the colleagues who've encouraged me to dream, test the limits, and joined me for too many sandwiches at Subway.

Asbury Theological Seminary—Florida Dunnam Campus students—partners in learning who come ripe from ministry, test our mutual discoveries outside the campus walls, then report back so we're all richer as a community.

Rudy & Faith Buettner—ministry partners who, many years ago, challenged me to jump headlong into marriage work. Rudy died after the first edition was published, but his prodding continues to live in my memory. Faith continues to challenge us.

Lyman Coleman—who taught me most everything I know about group life. As our pioneer, he taught us to connect our stories to God's story, before we knew it was so important. He took us back to Jesus' way of creating a Kingdom family, living richly with one another around the Scriptures.

Curt & Gina Deming—friends, colleagues, and members of our writing team who so willingly contributed to this book—birthed from the experiences of a rich marriage and a passionate commitment to the many young people they mentor and pastor.

Donald Joy—my mentor, teacher, and colleague. He early captured my imagination with God's Creation plan, and patiently nurtured as I grew. He's researched immensely and graciously shared what he's discovered.

Carolyn Smith—my life partner who, as a professional editor, has carried the weight of editing, designing, re-editing and keeping this project on track.

Jackie Truman—my former colleague on the Mentored Ministry team. She read most everything written here, encouraged me forward, and told me to stop cutting out parts she liked.

The ministry centers, like **Pearce Memorial Church**, **The Harbour Church**, and **The Orlando Fellowship** where we've learned, tested, and used what we teach.

Those not mentioned, who should be ... a HEARTY Thank You!

TO YOU

It's tough
for ministry leaders to
find guidance when walking in
and working through a
maze of relationship models—
particularly for marriages.

If you ever performed,
or plan to perform,
a wedding—
AND
you're committed to
helping couples experience
the adventure
of life-long marriage…

This book is to you!

Forward

When we helped plant a church in 2002, I was in for some surprises. I have been the teaching pastor of Melbourne Community Church since its founding. I expected weekly sermon preparation and pastoral ministry to the sick to become high priorities in my life, but I did not fully grasp the challenges of being an officer of a non-profit corporation. When our church added an administrator and associate pastor to our staff last year, I was excited for many reasons, and personally delighted to pass off some of my administrative responsibilities to our new staff members. On the other hand, marriage ministry has been an unexpected blessing of my pastoral ministry.

Marriage ministry at our church takes many forms. Three times in the last twelve years, I have done multi-week sermon series on marriage. My wife Gina and I have led three different marriage enrichment small groups. I officiate at lots of weddings, and my wife and I spend hours (usually 10-12) of pre-marital counseling with each couple to prepare for their marriage. It seems like we are always preparing for the next wedding. As I write this, we just finished doing two weddings and we are working with two more couples to prepare for weddings in the next six months.

My first wedding was in my pre-season as a pastor. I was ordained as a youth pastor, and our senior pastor told me that my ordination authorized me to "marry and bury." My family knew that I was ordained, and a distant cousin asked me to officiate at her wedding. Samantha and Bill were married at a golf course in South Florida, and it was the only wedding I've done in a robe rather than a suit. Priestly vestments are not the norm at our church; I'm still amused when I see the photos. I recall that we did a very brief marriage counseling meeting before the wedding. I cannot recall what we discussed, but I know that it was only one meeting. Bill and Samantha did not stay married long, and I felt that I had not helped them to prepare adequately.

When I became the teaching pastor of a new church plant, I knew that I needed to do better if I was going to be involved in marriage ministry. We planted Melbourne Community Church in November of 2002. Early in 2005, I was asked to officiate at my first "pastoral" wedding. Although I was in my forties, I was young in pastor years, and I knew that I needed help.

GETTING TRAINED

Friends of ours had recently married at a larger established church in our city, and they reported that the counseling had been very helpful. I contacted that church and asked if someone there would be available to coach me on their approach to pre-marital counseling. They graciously offered to help, and Gina and I met with a lay mentor couple from their church who led the pre-marital counseling ministry. They introduced us to a curriculum called FOCCUS published by Marriage Savers. We have mostly followed their advice, and we have used the FOCCUS material with 27 couples over the last ten years.

FOCCUS starts with an on-line survey completed by the engaged couple. Their responses form the framework for our discussions. We usually meet five or six times for about two hours over the course of several months. Most couples get at least 10 hours of pre-marital counseling before their wedding. Of the 27 couples we have counseled, two decided not to marry (which Marriage Savers views as a successful result of their program). One couple tabled their plans, and two are in process. Of the 22 couples who married, one couple is divorced, two are separated, and 19 seem to be thriving.

My first pastoral wedding set a pattern that has continued for 10 years. I am a bi-vocational pastor. I have been a high school history teacher for 26 years and a teaching pastor for 12 years. Over half of our weddings have involved at least one former student. These events are like mini-reunions, a sweet intersection of my two careers. At our last wedding a few weeks ago, the groom, three of four groomsmen, and several attendees were former students. At four of our weddings, both the bride and groom were former students.

LESSONS WE'VE LEARNED

Although it might seem like a long time, couples report back to us that the pre-marital counseling is beneficial and not overly burdensome. Pre-marital counseling is not optional if I'm going to officiate the wedding, but I have offered an "express lane" when needed.

We recommend early that the couples prioritize the marriage over the wedding. It helps to start the counseling early because it is easy to get distracted by the demands of the calendar as the wedding day approaches.

For couples who have the wherewithal to be indulgent, we recommend prioritizing the honeymoon over the wedding reception.

Studies show that the cost of the wedding is inversely proportional to the future success of the marriage, but that a honeymoon promotes the success of the marriage. That is why I recommend investing in the honeymoon rather than the reception.

A flawless ceremony is no predictor of marital success. At the rehearsal, I encourage the couple to develop the healthy habit of laughing off minor disappointments.

When I first started officiating at weddings, I naively expected that the local couples would be so appreciative that they would become regular members of our church. Of course many young couples today would prefer a traditional wedding, but do not see regular church attendance as an important habit (although it is another predictor of marriage success). Although I would prefer to see them regularly after the wedding, I'm still grateful for the opportunity to be involved in their weddings.

Marriage ministry has been an adventure. We have been generously blessed and creatively insulted. Since our non-denominational storefront church is not a particularly attractive venue, none of my weddings have been in my home church. I've done weddings in eight other churches, and a wide variety of other venues—hotels, restaurants, officers' clubs, parks and the beach.

OUR BEST WORK?

There is one piece of advice from our mentor couple coach that we have been slow to follow. They told us that we would not be able to keep up with marriage ministry ourselves. They said that we should train other couples to do the pre-marital counseling. We have been helped by one other couple. Jared and Sarah are both former students of mine. I met them both in my junior high history class in the 1990s, and they have been faithful friends since then. Jared is now our church's associate pastor and Sarah is our webmaster. They are available to help with pre-marital counseling, but Gina and I still do most of it ourselves. I don't think we're being stubborn here, but we find this part of our pastoral ministry to be very fulfilling and it seems successful.

I do not believe that couples come to us for pre-marital counseling because of our credentials or spiritual authority, but rather because of our marriage. They have often seen two negative examples: marriages that fail and marriages that merely survive because the couple is committed to upholding their vows. Gina and I just celebrated our 33rd anniversary. We are still pretty excited about our marriage, and it shows. I believe that is what the young couples are hoping for when they come to us. They don't want their marriages to fail, but they want a marriage that thrives, not one that lasts just because they are toughing it out and doing their duty.

Gina and I have a passion for marriage ministry. Because we married so young (and I still had a lot of growing up to do), our own marriage seems like an upset victory. We have seen the wreckage that results from failed marriages, so it feels like important to battle against that. We enjoy this part of our pastoral roles. Gina says it is the best ministry work we do. I think she would know, and I'm glad she thinks so.

—Curt Deming
Palm Bay, Florida

1

A Second Edition

I wonder what God had in mind setting Jesus up to perform his first miracle at a big Jewish wedding.[1] Actually it was Jesus' mother who pulled this one off.

You may know the story.

Jesus and a few of his followers were hanging out, enjoying the party when the wine ran out. What a huge embarrassment if you were the groom. The goal was to keep the guests happy from the beginning to the end of the celebration.

Why would Jesus' mother get involved? More importantly, why would she get Jesus involved? Why not let the groom's family go fetch more wine at the local grocery? The Scriptures give us no answer to those questions.

All we know is Jesus wanted to be left alone, but his mama refused to let him off the hook. And since she wouldn't take "no" for an answer, he decided to go all out. Not only did he turn six huge stone jugs of water into wine, he made the best wine anyone had ever tasted. It was so good that the host questioned the groom about bringing out the "good stuff" when the people were already tipsy.

Other than just throwing in an interesting story, why would this one make it into the Bible?

Does God want us to know that Jesus enjoyed great parties? Probably.

1 John 2:1–12

Does God want us to know that Jesus is concerned about the "regular" issues of daily life—those situations like the deep cultural embarrassment this groom and his family would have experienced when the wine jars ran empty? Without a doubt!

But might God's big point for a coming-out miracle at a wedding in Cana, be to demonstrate the value God places on marriages, even to providing the best wine for the occasion?

No cheap stuff for Jesus!

Though we'll discuss divorce—because it happens all too often—this is a book about launching healthy marriages for life.

Yet, when I ask pastors what they do to help couples prepare for great marriages, they usually look at their feet and respond with something like, "We try to do one or two counseling sessions with a couple before we perform the wedding."

Need I say it? That doesn't cut it.

I find that many pastors barely know the couples they officiate for.

It's time for a radical shift.

BEYOND WEDDINGS

Weddings are only one piece of a marriage. A very small piece when put into the perspective of a lifetime.

At the encouragement of my Asbury Theological Seminary—FLORIDA students, I pondered writing a book to help leaders increase the percentage of marriages that thrive for a lifetime. Our goal was to make it different than the marriage resources currently available.

The *first edition* was written more like a text for my students and anyone else who might have interest in weddings and marriages.

This *second edition* is totally rewritten, rearranged, and shortened. It's focused more directly toward ministry leaders; those leaders who are trying to make sense out of the changing relational landscape of the 21st century. Leaders who are committed to Jesus and people—no matter who those people are or where they come from. Leaders who ask questions but are not looking for simplistic answers.

This isn't meant as some high-brow theological discourse on marriage from a seminary professor, though any time we talk about

God we're doing theological reflection. And since I've now pastored for more than 40 years (from city streets to cement-columned church buildings) I don't have time for stuff that doesn't work. I'm committed to making anything I teach or write about, relevant for current ministry settings.

Though the original thought was to write a "how-to" book for weddings, we simply couldn't stop there. As we began working on this project, evaluating what we were creating (and using) in our own ministries, we reaffirmed that healthy marriages don't just happen in isolation. They are birthed in communities—*faith hothouses* where healthy marriages naturally grow in the rich soil of thriving relationships.

So we've merged **the how-to wedding notes** with **basic relationship understandings** into one vision. We imagine churches where children, youth, young adults, middle aged, and seniors, all live in vibrant interconnection with one another and with Jesus.

Churches still seem to provide the primary wedding venues and clergy are the most common officiates, so an increasing number of couples will turn up at our doors—people whom we've never met, who have no biblical or church knowledge—expecting us to perform their weddings.

At that point we have a list of choices.

We can *reject them,*

We can *go through the motions* just to get the wedding done, and make a little cash on the side, or

We can *set into motion a plan* that will transform a wedding day into the beginnings of a life-long marriage.

THE FLOW

The book is framed to flow from a biblical foundation through congregational applications to marriage/wedding-specific plans.

First we'll briefly build a biblical foundation through the lenses of creation, Jesus' teaching, Jesus' life, and the rest of the Scriptures. Next we'll review a few hot-topic issues that surface among relationship researchers.

From there we're ready to take the **big look** at how growing healthy relationships in our faith communities must be the *heart of our discipleship.*

With the **big look** in mind, we'll narrow the focus to see where weddings fit into the big picture. And finally we'll offer a detailed plan for you to adapt in your ministry setting.

I can almost hear you saying, "How much time do you think I have?"

So let me say it right up front. I know ministry leaders are not apathetic about marriages. What we are is just plain busy. And the thought of starting one more program probably makes the skin on your neck crawl.

This **isn't a new program**.

This is a new way of prioritizing what you're already committed to, so let's set the stage for your reading.

We assume that you, the reader, are a ministry leader of a faith community. If not, you'll need to translate the ideas to your ministry setting.

There is no need to reinvent the wheel. Most marriage ministry resources are available nearby.

You don't need a large congregation to have a great marriage ministry. You only need strong commitment and a simple plan to make a huge difference.

Marriage ministry is a team effort, not a solo act, so you'll need three or four people to join you.

Although you may create some new things, most of what will evolve in your marriage ministry plan is simply refocusing what you're already doing.

You'll get more sleep because you won't worry so much about the survival of marriages in your faith community.

By the time you finish reading, I hope when you hear the word "**wedding**," you'll think **life-long marriage**.

That's the goal!

We won't pretend to have all the answers. You already know that healthy relationships don't blossom magically. But we believe this book can become a practical tool for creating **your own** marriage ministry model—making an eternal difference in the lives of your people.

So as you read…

Dream big…

—Daryl L. Smith, Fall 2015

2

The Creation Dream

OUR FIRST THREE YEARS

Looking back some 42 years, it brings a chuckle. But at the moment it was serious.

On the second night of our honeymoon, I awoke in a cold-sweat panic. My mind was whirling at the thought, *I'm married! I have to take responsibility for this woman sleeping next to me.*

There's no way. I have enough trouble taking care of myself!

How could I afford it?

How can I possibly know the answer to all the questions that will come up?

How would I know how to tell her what to do?

How could I, the introverted wimp, be responsible for the future of this woman I loved?

I quickly considered several escape scenarios, but jumping from the lodge's second-floor window onto the lawn and then into icy Lake Superior didn't seem like the best idea.

I had come into our marriage with the understanding that I, as a man, was to lead our home—be the king of our castle.

I never thought of my father as an authoritarian husband, but everyone understood that Dad played the lead role. In reality, Mom and Dad never discussed issues in front of their children so they seemed to agree on most everything and get along well. Since I had never seen a woman in leadership, I bought into the idea that the world was "as it should be," a male dominated place.

My scriptural understanding of male-female relationships came mostly from male pastors who taught that biblical "headship" somehow carried the weight of authority and power. No one I knew ever dared challenge the few proof texts used to keep women in their place.

Yet, when my pre-life story was told it included the fact that Mom and Dad met in Texas, while Mom as the music minister, traveled with a female evangelist holding tent crusades. Imagine, in that culture, two women leading an amazing ministry. With that DNA in my veins, you'd think I'd have caught on more quickly.

But, no!

Fortunately, on that second honeymoon-night, God helped me calm down and remember that two evenings earlier we had *both* agreed to our vows. We had *both* committed to work at this life together. And we were in it *together* for the long haul. I breathed deeply, finally fell back to sleep, and kept that fearful secret from Carolyn for several years.

I never felt comfortable playing my assumed role as lord of the family, even though I worked at it really hard.

I struggled. I discussed. I looked at the Bible.

When I began intense Bible study with friends, my preconceptions began to lose their footing. I started to ponder the possibility that my identity didn't rest on my dominance of our couplehood.

A BIBLICAL FOUNDATION

When God created humanity "in our own image,"[1] God had a bigger dream than objects of entertainment or children to look after. God made humans, male and female, and envisioned them in a glorious one-ness relationship—with God and one another. The pinnacle of that relationship between the humans was in a covenant called marriage. And a life-model for God's entire family—the church

I wish someone had told us the truth before that panicked honeymoon night or before the "I dos" at the altar. I wish we had known that the character of our relationship was rooted in our misconceived

1 Genesis 1:26 (NLT).

notions about marriage and relationships, and our conceptions were neither healthy nor biblical.

Our work with couples we guide into marriage is shaped by our theology. If our theology is biblically sound then our marriage ministry can be sound. If our theology is weak, then our marriage ministry will be deformed by a "naturalistic fallacy"[2]—believing what we've seen in our experience of marriages is how male-female relationships should be.

The key to a truly biblical foundation is filtering our theology
first through the lens of creation,
then the lens of Jesus' teachings
then the lens of Jesus' life example,
and finally the lens of the Scriptures as a whole.

Through those lenses we'll get the close-up view of God's original plan—the plan that God called "excellent in every way."[3]

The plan that creates great relationships and excellent marriages.

Genesis Chapter 1 sings us an amazing creation song, climaxing in the splendor of God's best work—Woman and Man, created in God's image. Chapter 2 fills in the blanks from a different perspective. Chapter 3 tells of the awful unraveling that resulted when we humans decided to go it alone.

From that time forward, we have seemed bent on distorting God's excellent plan. We've used generations of sinful action (what "is") to justify our grasping for authority, forcing others, especially our women, into submission as we attempt to play God. Only God can be God. No human was designed for that role. So any time we lord it over another human we can be certain that we've gotten mixed up on who we are and what we are created for. We are called to a partnership of equals living in deep relationship with one another and with God.

THE CREATION SONG

From the beginning of Genesis chapter 1, God proclaims the worlds and creatures into existence.

2   A "naturalistic fallacy" is a false idea that is assumed to be true based on the way the world or a particular situation is witnessed to be. The idea is that because things "are" a certain way, they are as God intended them to be. However, this fallacy leaves no place for the resurrected Jesus or the Holy Spirit's transforming work.
3   Genesis 1:31 (TLB)

But Chapter 1 verse 26 presents a hauntingly strange phrase that brings the whole story to a pause.

"Then God said, 'Let us make people in our image, to be like ourselves. They will be masters over all life—the fish in the sea, the birds in the sky, and all the livestock, wild animals, and small animals.' So God created people in his own image; God patterned them after himself; male and female he created them…. Then God looked over all he had made, and he saw that it was excellent in every way."[4]

"Let *us*…" The Trinity—Father, Son and Holy Spirit—gathered to discuss the next step—the final act of creation.[5] We'll never know if they had previously spoken of this final stage. Perhaps this was the culmination of an ongoing discussion that is not recorded. Or, maybe the author wants us to catch our breath and pay close attention to what's coming. Whatever the reason, it's clear something of extreme import was up. This was the big climax. You can almost hear the crescendoing tympani roll coming across the universe.

God, the Trinity, finished their creation song with a spectacular formation (Hebrew: *adam*), coming up out of the regular stuff of earth (Hebrew: *adamah*). These creatures were unlike anything preceding them. They were molded into the reflection of God, with all the splendor that invokes,[6] and filled to the brim with the breath of God. Then the *adam*—both male and female together—were launched upon the earth with God's grand blessing and a directive to go forth, multiply (bear children) and co-steward all creation.[7]

Dr. Joseph Coleson points to the truth we might miss here.

Both female and male are ʻ*adam*. Both male and female are created by God. Both female and male are in the image of God….The female

4 Genesis 1:26–27, 31 (NLT).

5 For further study, note that the ancient Hebrew authors would not have been thinking in terms of Trinity. It is our later understanding that projects Trinitarian models back into the early Scriptures.

6 Coleson, Joseph E., *ʻEzer Cenegdo: A Power Like Him, Facing Him as Equal*, 3rd Ed. (Grantham, PA: Wesleyan/Holiness Women Clergy, 1996), p. 4.

7 Also, Genesis 1:27, the author drives home the significant point of this event by using a Hebrew word for *creation*, rarely used in the rest of the Bible. And he uses it three times. "God *created* the human, in the image of God He *created* it; male and female He *created* them." See Coleson, p. 4–5.

is not a part of creation over which the male has dominion...." In fact, "for one half of humanity to subjugate the other half robs both of God's intended blessing upon all humans.[8]

And Dr. Michael Lawler adds,

"We, in Hebrew 'adam, in English *humankind*, came from God. Male and female as we are, we are from God, and together we make up humankind. This fact alone, that God names woman and man together 'adam, established the equality of men and women as human beings."[9]

Lest we get it wrong, the author gives it to us again in Genesis 5:1–2: "This is the written account of the descendants of Adam. When God created human beings [*adam*], he made them to be like himself. He created them male and female, and he blessed them and called them human [*adam*]."[10]

MARRIAGE IS BORN

The authors of Genesis could not let this startling story end on a two-verse cadence at the climax of the creation song. Thus Chapter 2 opens another perspective of this amazing event. In Chapter 1, the "creation of the 'adam—the human pair—is climactic. In the Chapter 2 account of creation, the differentiation of the 'adam into male and female is climactic."[11]

Until the *adam*, God created by speaking life into existence. By contrast, God becomes intimately involved in the creation of humans, forming *adam* out of *adamah* (smallest dust particles of earth; ground) and breathing life into them. Unlike the terse style of Chapter 1, where the word *adam* is attached to both male and female, in the first part of Chapter 2 the term *adam* refers to "the human."[12] Despite our

8 Coleson, p. 7.

9   Lawler, Michael G., "Perichoresis: New Theological Wine in an Old Theological Wineskin, *Horizons*, 22/1 (1995), p. 57.

10 NLT, emphasis added.

11 Coleson, p. 10.

12 Norman J. Cohen in *Self, Struggle and Change: family conflict stories in Genesis and their healing insights for our lives* (Woodstock, VT: Jewish Lights Publishing, 1995) quotes ancient rabbinic teachers who describe this original human in terms of a two-faced being—looking in opposite directions. When the woman and man are separated out of the original

uneasiness with the word, the human has no gender and could best be described as an "it" until God does the bifurcation surgery.[13] From that one being, God differentiates the human into a female and a male.

The terms "Adam" and "Eve" should never be used for humans until after Genesis 3:20, as they are terms coming out of the Fall.

Once the human (*'adam*) is formed and placed in the garden, it is given direction for eating, not eating, and what tasks to perform. At this point (verse 18), as if in an aside to the on-looking audience of creatures, God gives us a clue to what is coming. Before the human has caught on, God declares, "It is not good for the human to be alone. I will make it a partner." The Hebrew term here, sometimes translated "helper," is not one of inferiority or that of an apprentice, as one might suspect. It is the same word used to describe *God* as our helper or rescuer. In this context the terminology implies that this "helper" will rescue the human. This companion-to-come is to be a full partner in the best sense of the word.

Then, as if to give the human a clearer picture of its dilemma, God brings before it the other created beings and asks the human to provide names (labels of sorts). As the naming draws to a close, the human recognizes that each creature has a mate—one of its kind. But for the human there is not one of its kind.

In the middle of verse 21 the light finally dawns. The human gets the picture God had in mind from the beginning. God had not forgotten to finish creation. God had not forgotten to make a mate. It's as if God the Trinity wanted the human to understand that it was created for something more than itself or the other created beings. The human was created for miraculous relationships in the image of God, the Trinity.

But the human cannot solve its own problem; it cannot create its own mate. God must complete the creation process. And the human cannot conceive of the surprise that is to come.

So in a deep sleep, under the surgical knife of God, two new beings emerge from the single human.

Woman and Man.

Ishsha and *Ish*.

human, both are brought back together as two individuals, standing face to face, demonstrating their oneness and co-regency.

13 Coleson, pp. 13–14.

Life-long relational partners like no other creatures.
Both created in the image of God.
Both inbreathed with the breath of God.
Both blessed as stewards of all creation.
LET THE TRUMPETS SOUND!

Upon awakening, the now differentiated male is so shocked by who stands at the foot of the surgical bed that he can only gasp, "Wow! This is just like me. In fact she is part of me."

God took content from the human's side—men don't bother counting your ribs, they're all there—and created Woman. Then closing the side, the remaining creation is Man.

We were told earlier that the *adam* (the human) was formed out of *adamah* (earth's smallest particles, the dust of the ground).[14] Now in the description of God's surgical work we note the amazing fact that "no new material, not even additional dust particles/atoms, were added…. This is (the) sexual differentiation"[15] of the original human. Both woman and man brought forth from the original human.

The GRAND CLIMAX of creation!

With God the Trinity as the officiate, the first wedding is performed with the final proclamation, "It is so good, so very good!"[16] So every time we observe a couple standing face to face, reciting their marriage vows, we replay this original grand scenario. And all creation longs for the mirror image of that day—the day scripture foretells at the end of time—the marriage feast when Jesus, the groom, gathers his church, the bride, and all creation will join in its restoration.

As men and women we are designed to experience a oneness like the Trinity itself experiences. For those of us who remain single, Jesus rounds out the story: "For where two or three come together in my

---

14 When the nuclear physicists were looking for a word to express the smallest form of matter, they looked back to *adamah*, arriving at the word *atom*.

15 Joy, Donald M. and Robbie B., *Two Become One: God's Blueprint for Couples*, (Nappanee, IN: Evangel Publishing House, 2002), p. 27. An earlier edition of this book was published under the title, *Lovers—Whatever Happened to Eden?*, copyright © 1987 by Donald M. Joy.

16 Genesis 1:31 (MSG)

name, there am I with them"[17] That's oneness; that's intimate community. A husband and wife model what God intends as the pattern for the whole of God's Kingdom family.

LIFE IN COMMUNITY

Joseph Coleson describes the dramatic difference between God's plan and societal life as the ancients understood it (see Genesis 2:24). "In the patriarchal societies of ancient western Asia, a man did not leave his father and his mother; he brought his wife to live with him under his father's authority."[18] Not so in this radically different model for families and relationships.

> "God did not intend women to be the servants and breeding stock of a male-dominated extended family. God did intend every woman to be the co-equal partner with her new husband in the new, independent household they establish together.... God did intend husband and wife to rejoin as one flesh...what God had differentiated in the final creative act, the act by which God provided for human community upon the earth in reflection of divine community in heaven."[19]

In Mark 10:5–9, Jesus challenged the taunting religious leaders to get it right. Speaking of Moses' allowance for divorce, Jesus responded:

> "He wrote this commandment only as a concession to your hard hearts. But 'God made them male and female' from the beginning of creation. 'This explains why a man leaves his father and mother and is joined to his wife, and the two are united into one.' Since they are no longer two but one, let no one split apart what God has joined together." (NLT)

On the night of Jesus' betrayal he drew the final marriage analogy to the faith community. He demonstrated how this life of mutual service should be carried out by pulling off his cloak, wrapping a towel around his waist, grabbing the basin of water, dropping to his knees and washing his disciples' feet. The disciples has just been bickering about who would be the greatest in God's Kingdom so Jesus gave them

---

17 Matthew 18:20 (NIV)
18 Coleson, p. 19.
19 Colson p. 19.

the serving lesson of a life-time.

From our Western mindsets, with the monarchical influence of presidents, kings, popes and bishops, we tend to think with a verticalized concept of leadership; thus tending to view the Trinity as a hierarchy. We then wrongly transfer that concept into our marriage relationships.[20] From our vantage point we question, maybe doubt, the real possibility for two humans to truly become one in the image of God. And to carry the logic forward, if two can never be one, how can a whole community become one?

These questions are not new. The earliest Christians wrestled with these issues. Yet, since humans are created in the image of God, it's imperative that we look at all of our relationships in Trinitarian terms. As we seek to understand how two can become one, we must attempt to get our minds around a Trinitarian concept of marriage. Then we can extend our understanding of the deeper marriage-symbolism into our current faith communities and on to the end of time when Jesus and His Church are united for eternity.

Obviously we can never truly comprehend three persons as one. Some have tried to describe this three-person-of-the-Trinity relationship as "the Dance of God"—all beings moving together in intimate relationship, yet each maintaining their personhood. You may have seen the wonderful painting *The Old Testament Trinity* by Andrei Rublev[21] that attempts to capture in oils what we can only play with in our imaginations.

Most importantly, at that moment of gender differentiation, when God created *Woman* and *Man,* it was not a differentiation for aloneness. Through the bifurcation surgery God declared that as the Trinity lives in community, so are humans to live in community—in a place of oneness.

---

20 Moltmann, Jürgen, *The Trinity and the Kingdom: The Doctrine of God* (Minneapolis: Fortress Press, 1993), p. 19ff. Moltmann lays out this thesis of cultural hierarchicalism "invading" the Western church in chapter 6, "The Kingdom of Freedom."

21 Rublev, Andrei, "The Old Testament Trinity," a painting in Tretyakov Gallery, Moscow, Russia.

THE GOOD MARRIAGE GOES BAD

When we step into Genesis chapter 3, the dream story bursts like a carnival balloon, into thin air. It's a familiar story—both from history and all too often our present. God gave humans the choice. Man and woman could either live within the boundaries of their creator or attempt to assemble life without the directions. The first woman and first man took the second option, took the bite of forbidden fruit and decided to go it on their own. The sound of that single bite must have echoed across the garden, followed by a giant gasp and then a deathly silence. In that fateful moment the awful consequences began to unfold.

Immediately the man and the woman were quite literally caught with their pants down. They hurriedly looked around and began gathering anything that might make clothing. They were ashamed of their nakedness—the same nakedness that they celebrated on their wedding day.

Stuart Briscoe[22] suggests that they were not so much embarrassed by the nakedness they saw in each other as by the reality of their differences. Those differences reminded them that they were uniquely made, and made for each other. As the awesome handiwork of God, created for *interdependence* with one another and with God, they now declared independence from God, which resulted in independence from one another. They were left standing alone, self-dependent and inadequate for the task. They couldn't face that tragic reality. So, they covered it up.

Yet, they couldn't hide from God.

We cannot imagine the horror Man and Woman experienced when God confronted them. There they stood, naked before the One who had declared them excellent in every way, trying to hide their reproductive parts from the one who had created those parts, and had commissioned them to reproduce.

How absurd!

How gruesomely painful!

It was worse than getting your hand caught in the eternal cookie

---

22 Briscoe, D. Stuart, *Communicators Commentary: Genesis*, Lloyd J. Oglivie, Ed. (Waco: Word Books, 1987), p. 65.

jar. And we can only imagine the pain-filled grief that God the Trinity experienced in that horrific moment.

Then God the Trinity faced the unimaginable task of pronouncing the consequences of the woman's and man's sin. The words must have seared as God leveled curses at the serpent and the ground. To the man and the woman—the made-in-God's-image creatures—God announced, *not* curses, but unavoidable consequences.

To the woman:
"As a consequence of your actions,
 I will increase your suffering—the pain of childbirth
And the sorrow of bringing forth the next generation.
 You will desire your husband; *but rather than a companion,*
He will be the dominant partner."[23]

In other words, her first instinct to worship God would be perverted. She would now look to her man as her god. Not only would this idolatry draw her away from God, it would reinforce her husband's desire to play god.

For men, the thought of a woman's worship sounds absolutely wonderful. In reality it has caused immense pain for both women and men across the centuries. Women tend to carry an umbilical-cord attachment to their man, even in the face of abuse. Women have suffered under the dictatorial hand of their men; often because the men wrongly interpreted God's statement as giving them permission to enforce submission. And we men risk cardiac arrest under the stress of attempted godhood.

To the man:
"Because you followed your wife's advice
instead of My command and ate of the tree
From which I had forbidden you to eat, cursed is the ground.
For the rest of your life,
You will fight for every crumb of food
from the *crusty clump of* clay *I made you from.*"[24]

---

23 See Genesis 3:16, *The Voice Bible,* Copyright ©2012, Thomas Nelson, Inc. The Voice™ translation, ©2012, Ecclesia Bible Society. All rights reserved.
24 See Genesis 3:17–18, *The Voice Bible,* The Voice™ translation.

Nothing would come easy for him and he would wear his knuckles bare trying to make the world subject to his wishes. He would never conquer the work world because it would always prove resistant and sap him dry. "What man might have been and how he might have been transported from this scene we can only conjecture, but what he became and what he heads toward is all too clear as a visit to many a factory floor or cemetery will readily testify."[25]

Chapter 3 verse 20, brings the final act of sabotage. In a statement of dominion and power over the woman, the man takes for *himself* the name *adam*—stealing the name given to both woman and man to-gether—the name of ultimate dignity and worth. He declares himself Adam and the woman he names Eve, or child bearer. Just as the human had named the animals, the man took lordship over the woman by naming her as well. Instead of co-stewardship as God had directed, the man took the authority for himself and demoted the woman to the status of other created beings. And instead of an exalted name, he gives her a functionary name. From now on her value would come as the incubator of humanity; one who births and nurses.

From the pinnacle of creation, our foreparents have fallen into the sin-filled pit. The man and woman broke relationship with God, de-stroyed their relationship with each other—and sin entered the world. The man took the authority of God and the woman became an object for use. Mercifully, God didn't abandon them in their brokenness—refusing to let them live forever in their sin. He banished them, away from the "tree of life," sending them out from the garden of wonderful beginnings to an uncertain and grief-filled future.

A REDEMPTIVE EXAMPLE

When I read the biblical story of Jacob, Rachel and Leah, it takes my breath away.[26] Leah was the unwanted bride. Jacob loved and intended to marry her sister Rachel. After a night in his wedding bed, Jacob awoke to the shock of finding Leah. Deceived by a conniving father-in-law anxious to marry off his oldest daughter, Jacob had slept with the wrong woman. When he finally did marry the younger sister, his

---

25 Briscoe, *Communicator's Commentary: Genesis*, p. 66.

26 To get the entire story, you need to read Genesis chapters 27–35.

chosen bride, Leah was left in dismay.

As a woman in the lineage of Eve, Leah knew that her value depended upon her ability to please Jacob with a child, particularly a boy child. As we pick up the story in Genesis 29:31 the scripture is plain.

Leah was not loved.

She was strictly an incubator for potential sons. And she did bear sons. Each time she gave birth, she echoed the message of women before her, "Surely my husband will love me now." Her *umbilical cord* of "desire for her husband" as described in Genesis 3:16 caused her to keep striving for Jacob's love.

Yet, after three sons, she was no better off.

In Genesis 29:35 the picture abruptly changes. Instead of again begging for Jacob's love—the god who doesn't respond—she turned her face to the Lord God. In a moment of faith she proclaims, "This time I will praise the Lord."

For this one moment in history she broke free from worshipping her man to worshipping God. And in her celebration she birthed a fourth son and named him, *Judah!*

That should take your breath away!

This child, birthed while praising God, becomes the namesake for the ruling tribe of the Israeli nation.

He is the forbearer of the historic King David.

This is the linage through whom Jesus came.[27]

The Lion of Judah—Name above All Names, at the end of time.[28]

Leah chose to escape the Fall's damage and, in that marvelous moment, her story became immersed in God's amazing redemption story.

GOD NEVER GIVES UP

Let's move forward a few thousand years.

God had too much invested in humanity to ever give up. So in a final move against evil, the Trinity agreed on the appointed time for final victory. One of the three must visit, in person, what C.S. Lewis called the "silent planet."[29] They must take on their own shoulders the

---

27 For example, Hebrews 7:14.

28 For example, Revelation 5:5.

29 Lewis, C.S., *Out of the Silent Planet* (NY: MacMillan Co., 1965).

do-and-die risk for humanity's salvation.

According to the Apostle Paul, "…when the set time had fully come…"[30] Jesus arrived on the scene as God's ultimate love-invitation—to model and live God's love in human skin. He came to exemplify God's plan for life and relationships; to invite us back home from our wandering.

I'd never noticed the power of this passage until Dr. Zaida Maldonado Perez[31] preached from Luke 11:27–28, in our campus chapel. She pointed out that as Jesus was in heated debate with the religious leaders, a woman in the crowd was so overjoyed by this new teacher that she couldn't help herself. She exclaims, "Blessed is the mother who gave you birth and nursed you." As a woman growing up in the Jewish culture she knew the rules; she understood her value. There was no greater praise that she could pronounce on Jesus' mother than that she had birthed and nursed well.

To our shock however, Jesus doesn't buy into her praise. In fact, he rebukes her. He shouts back, "Blessed rather are those who hear the word of God and obey it."[32] In other words, "No, woman! Never again will my mother or you or any other woman be valued for what they can produce by pleasing their husbands through childbearing. You will, from now on, find your value in following and obeying me."

Wow!

With one stroke of his verbal pen he signed a release order for all women and all men, for all time. He denounced the result of sin in the garden and proclaimed a new day in his Kingdom. Jesus set the whole Jewish religious world reeling. Now women (the oppressed) and men (the oppressors) were liberated to live-into God's creation story.

THE SPIRIT-EMPOWERED POSSIBILITIES

But Jesus came for more than foot washing and teaching powerful lessons. He was not just another good man, wandering the hills of Judea

---

30 Galatians 4:4.

31 Dr. Zaida Maldonado Perez is Professor of Church History and Theology, Asbury Theological Seminary—Florida Dunnam Campus, Orlando, FL. She regularly preaches in the campus chapel and around the world.

32 See Luke 11:27–28 (NIV).

looking for a truth-starved crowd. Better than the 11 o'clock news, the greatest news ringing clear from the New Testament and down the halls of history is that Jesus' love took him from an upper room in Jerusalem to death on a cross—wiping out sin, to a glorious resurrection—giving us eternal life, and then to heaven—his Spirit coming to reside in us.

If Jesus' death and resurrection were real ... if the Holy Spirit was actually released at Pentecost to reside in human beings ... then we 21st century humans may also return from the pit of sin.

We are no longer captive to the naturalistic fallacy that says "the way things are is the way they were intended to be." God never intended us to live in broken relationships; to coerce and abuse one another. God desires that we live radically differently from the "way things are." We are purposed for a life empowered by the Spirit of Christ.

So, whether out of ignorance or willfulness—any time we take authoritarian roles in our family, we've replaced God with self-idolatry.

Whenever we teach (or live out) the inequality of men and women in our ministries, we are teaching and living sin.[33] The same sin that Jesus came to redeem us from and sent the Holy Spirit to empower us to live apart from.

Yet, as our marriages are centered on Jesus—as we let God be the leader of our families and us the followers, serving one another—we can truly know the joy of a partnership better than that of the first man and first woman. Just as God walked in the garden beside the first man and woman, today God's Spirit desires to reside *within* each woman and man—recreating our relationships into God's creation-dream from before the dawn of time.

A DREAM:

Where both male and female demonstrate their special attributes of the nature of God...

Where leadership is shared in the home kingdom—using the gifts that God plants in each individual...

Where both a man and woman give themselves wholly in service to each other and to God...

33 Coleson, p. 37.

That truly fulfills the deep and eternal longing planted in Woman and Man on that first surgical table in the garden…

That provides a powerful parable for all who are searching for a way to *get it right* in love, marriage, and ministry.

3

The Big Picture

The only way a church can develop an excellent marriage ministry is by conceptualizing a life-span approach for the persons they minister to. For example, the local church needs to examine what it is doing to prepare young and singles for healthy dating and eventual marriage. A premarital education program is crucial. We believe every church should have a marriage mentoring ministry. With its boomerang effect, marriage mentoring strengthens newlyweds as well as more seasoned couples. The crucial years of beginning a family must be given more attention, as should the empty nest syndrome (where our nation is seeing a spike in the divorce rate).[1]

To assume that Marriage Ministry is something we only do in a couple of counseling sessions before a wedding is to miss the point. Not only

1 Les Parrott III and Leslie Parrott, "The SYMBIS Approach to Marriage Education," *Journal of Psychology and Theology*, 2003, 31, 3, 210.

are we short-changing the couples we guide to marriage, our congregations will never get to the deeper levels of healthy relationships that are called for in Christian community.

THE ATMOSPHERE

Christian Formation is the atmosphere for growing healthy relationships.

As females and males we are created with a mysterious interlock between personhood and *spirithood*. To speak of our spiritual life is to also speak of our personhood.

Our goal then is to help people experience "the process of being conformed to the image of Christ for the sake of others."[2] As the Holy Spirit grows individuals more into the image of Jesus, congregations will also grow into healthier communities.

What if we taught our children to live in healthy relationships with one another, with adults and in their families? What if teens and young adults understood the reality of mutual respect for one another as they begin partnering off? What if our divorcees, widows/widowers, blended families, and single parents were cared for in a community where they could learn to rebuild their lives in new and biblical ways? What if grandparents and parents understood their powerful mentoring impact on children and teens? What if our church staff team deeply loved one another and expressed it publicly? What if our governing board and the pastoral staff saw themselves as partners in ministry—committed to the care of one another?

You get the point.

The answer to that list of questions really gets to the heart of what it is to live like Jesus. Dr. Bob Mulholland offers this definition of Spiritual Formation:

The process—it's on-going and growing.

Of being conformed—reshaped, made into something new.

To the image of Christ—this is no ordinary shape. This is the image of the Creator who planted the original image in us and breathed our lungs full of the breath of life.

---

2 Mulholland, Jr., M. Robert, *Invitation to a Journey: A Road Map for Spiritual Formation*, (Downers Grove, IL: IVPress, 1993) , p. 19.

For the sake of others—It's not about us. We're to be shaped like Jesus so his love flows through us and others' lives are transformed.

If loving relationships were modeled in our congregations, divisions would be a thing of the past. Our children would grow up in an atmosphere of respect, love, and care. Our young adults walking the marriage aisle would arrive better prepared for marriage and enjoy the life-long support of their faith community.

THE CORE FORMATIONAL TOOL

Formational communities (small groups, Village Groups)[3] are to be *the core of ministry*. They should never be an appendage added to an already program-filled ministry.

Instead of creating a cluster of new small groups, you can start with existing small groups (you may call them boards, committees, classes, etc.). As you intentionally grow them into Village Groups, they will become the way people are cared for, where people grow as Jesus-followers, and the way God's mission/ministry gets done inside and outside the church walls.

For example, the next time you struggle during a board meeting, think how differently the board members would behave if they had spent time pouring their lives into one another before starting the business session. Just imagine more work getting done and fewer issues to argue over.

Then as you recognize needs that are not met or people who are not connected in community, you will begin training new leaders and creating new groups.[4]

As Village Groups become a way of life for all ages, in all ministry settings, Christian Formation will become the congregational atmosphere. The result—a healthy community.

---

3 I'll use the term I prefer, *Village Groups,* throughout the remainder of this book because it denotes a safe and healthy place to grow. The term *small groups* often evokes a negative response from people.

4 For help on turning your current boards, committees, and teams into Village Groups or starting and leading new Village Groups, check out our new book *The End of Small Groups: Leading Incarnational Villages* (Amazon, 2015).

It's About Story

There's not room to discuss Village Groups at length in this book but here are a couple of brief guidelines.

First, Village Groups come to life when they spend less time in *in-depth* Bible study and more time in relationship-building on a scriptural foundation. Sometime this is called Inductive Bible Study. It's where people *jump into the Bible* story and look around for themselves. To see where they fit.

Too often people call for more *in-depth* Bible study because they'd rather dig out scriptural facts than learn to live with their brothers and sisters of the faith community. The truth is, we cannot learn *social values*—and every biblical value is a social value—unless we try it out in a safe, small communities.[5]

Second, we must never short-change our people by letting them substitute biblical knowledge for a deeper immersion in the Scriptures. When God's story (the Bible), My story, and Your story intersect, amazing community blossoms. Jesus said that he shows up when two or three (or more) people gather in his name.[6] That's when a transformed and healthy community forms—filled with people who look a whole lot like Jesus.

Set Goals

Once we are committed to creating the proper Atmosphere (Christian Formation) and the Core Formational Tool (Village Groups), we should create a list of specific goals. This may get you started:

As ministry leaders:

1. We will lead our congregations by intentionally focusing on healthy relationships at every level.
2. We will create new Village Groups (4–12 people) of care, study, and mission as we see needs arise.
3. We will start turning our current boards, committees, teams, etc., into Village Groups.
5. We will probably create several new "events" to raise the relational focus—such as an *engaged weekend.*

---

5 For more about the importance of community life for learning social values (values of relating to other people) check out the research of Lev Vygotsky.

6 Matthew 18:20.

6. We will create an intentional strategy for couple care.
7. We will nurture our children, teens, and young adults so they are better prepared for a life-long marriage.

A REFERENCE POINT

The following chart shows a broad-spectrum marriage-ministry model. It is only a sample of the many possibilities for growing (and caring for) people in all life stages. Don't panic that you cannot create or manage every listed program.

DON'T EVEN TRY!

That's not the idea. Make it a starting point.

Certainly, you will notice gaps that need filling in your ministry setting. The key is for people, from the youngest to the oldest ages, to learn to work on relationships across the span of the faith community, both males and females, both children and adults…for all seasons of life.

As you look at the chart, you'll want to dream about creating your own ministry design. Here are some questions to ask yourself:

1. What are the relational needs of our congregation and community?
2. Who do we know that is willing and committed to guide a specific ministry?
3. What are *one* or *two* areas where we can effectively begin, because we have the people, and they have the passion to pull it off?
4. Which needs do our people have that must be met by partnering with other ministry groups who already provide the resources?

Remember, you should NOT create or offer every ministry on the sample chart. You and your people must decide where God wants you to focus your energy, then go for it, creating your own chart.

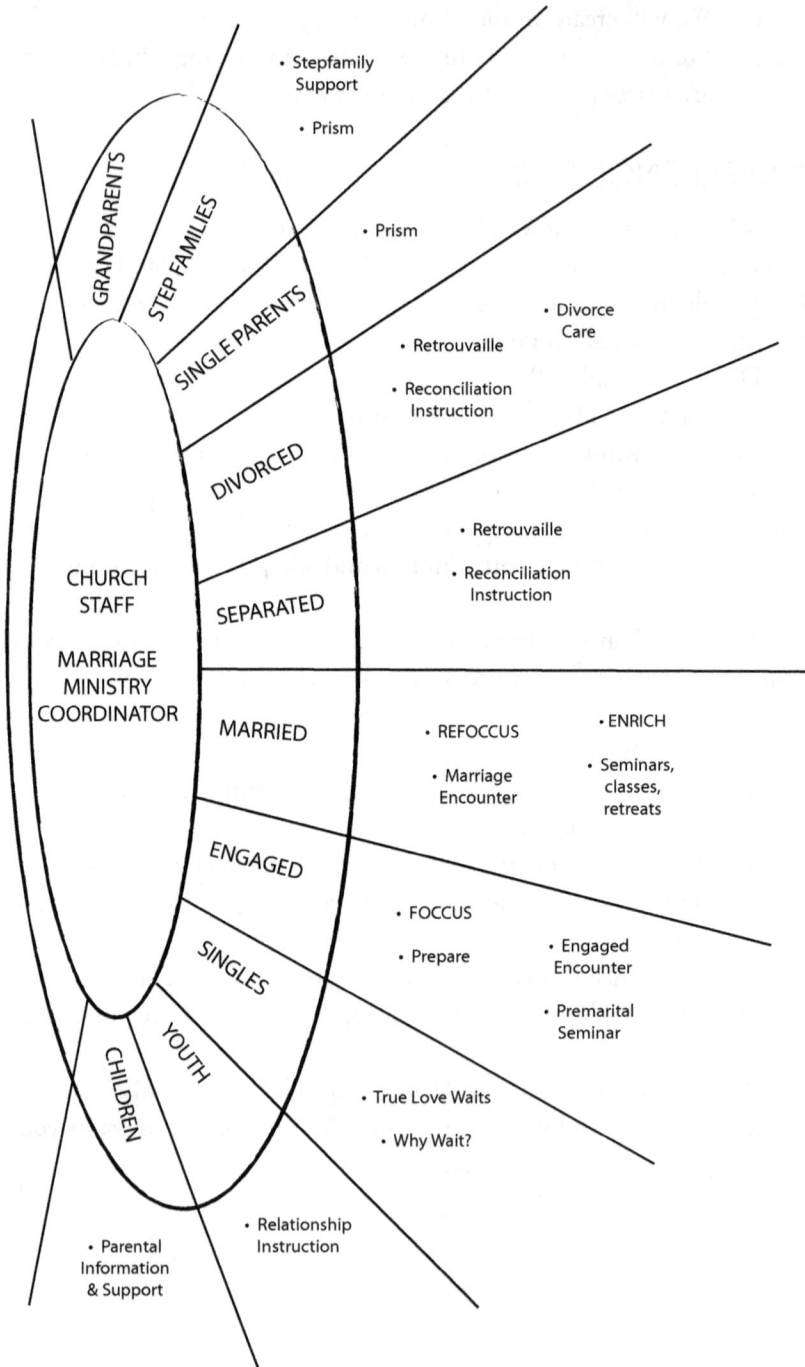

GRANDPARENTS

STEP FAMILIES

SINGLE PARENTS

DIVORCED

SEPARATED

MARRIED

ENGAGED

SINGLES

YOUTH

CHILDREN

CHURCH
STAFF

MARRIAGE
MINISTRY
COORDINATOR

- Stepfamily
  Support
- Prism

- Prism

- Divorce
  Care
- Retrouvaille
- Reconciliation
  Instruction

- Retrouvaille
- Reconciliation
  Instruction

- REFOCCUS   - ENRICH
- Marriage   - Seminars,
  Encounter   classes,
                  retreats

- FOCCUS
- Prepare   - Engaged
                  Encounter
                - Premarital
                  Seminar

- True Love Waits
- Why Wait?

- Relationship
  Instruction
- Parental
  Information
  & Support

WORK FROM THE MIDDLE

Every time we stand at the marriage altar with an engaged couple, we stand at the center-point between creation and an eternal wedding feast. We are re-creating a dramatic vision of healthy relationships lived in community, affirming God's plan for a life-long marriage. And we are offering hope to those living with broken or mending relationships.

With that mid-point in mind we work back toward children and youth to help them come to the model marriage. Obviously, there is no perfect marriage, but we must arouse a dream as the target for which to aim. Simultaneously we work forward to strengthen marriages, to restore broken marriages, to bring reconciliation to damaged relationships, to assist blended families, and to help grandparents learn to effectively impact those who are younger.

WITH CHILDREN

It's never too early to help children learn to create healthy relationships with persons of both genders. Human relationships are the physical connector to a *God-relationship* for children.

This is not the place for a lesson on child development and how you should run your children's ministry. However, you can assist children, beginning in the nursery, using what you already have in place, and adding to it where needed.

Help Kids Put Words to It

Before they know the words, children are building pictures of God and relationships. Walter Wangerin Jr. paints this profound word picture to illustrate.

> *Who can say when, in any child, the dance with God begins? No one. Not even the child can later look back and remember the beginning of it, because it is as natural an experience (as early and as universally received) as the child's relationship with the sun or with his bedroom. And the beginning, specifically, cannot be remembered because in the beginning there are no words for it. The language to name, contain, and to explain the experience comes afterward....*

And then there comes the time when the child awakens to the dance. He becomes aware of his own experience.... First there is the reality; and then there comes the personal consciousness of that reality; he consciously makes room for it in his existence....

But then—in order for the first passage of faithing to be fully accomplished, effectively to lead thereafter into the second passage—there must occur one more evolvement of the dance.... His trust in his own perceptions diminishes. His babyish names and stories for his experience with the Dear Almighty come under harsher judgment; they are in peril of becoming fairytales, products of a child's imagination, which one puts away with childish things.

Now, finally, language must perform it second function—explaining and containing—in order that the experience be confirmed, preserved: confessed! And so the dance may continue in spite of his maturer world.[7]

Children first encounter God **between 18 months and three years of age**.

Read that again. It's true.

It's never too early to start our ministry with children.

As adults, we can help children put language to the mystery that's going on inside. They need to hear (and act out) the stories of Jesus—to begin "naming" the mystery of their experience. Rather than condemning them—as sinners needing to "get saved"—children should be encouraged to respond to God's love that is already at work within them (Wesleyan theologians call it prevenient grace). Jesus never condemned anyone.[8] His only word was good news to any who responded to his love.

---

7   *The Orphean Passages* by Walter Wangerin, Jr. (Grand Rapids: Zondervan, 1996) 20-22.

8   Yes, Jesus did condemn the rule-pushing church leaders for keeping people from God's kingdom purposes. But the Apostle John gives us God's plan for recovering His family: "This is how much God loved the world: He gave his Son, his one and only Son. And this is why: so that no one need be destroyed; by believing in him, anyone can have a whole and lasting life. God didn't go to all the trouble of sending his Son merely to point an accusing finger, telling the world how bad it was. He came to help, to put the world right again." (John 3:16-17, MSG).

Take Exceptional Care of the Nursery

At one of my first ministry interviews, the nursery director pointedly reminded me that the nursery is the most important ministry in a congregation.

I agree!

Nursery workers, along with parents, offer God's love in human touch[9] to children who are just discovering whether the world is a safe and loving place. And since both men and women demonstrate their particular flavor of God's image, we must always include both women and men, working together with children. Children need to experience human love and God's love from both genders.

In my mental ear I can almost hear you protesting. I know the horror stories of sexual abuse with children. I train students on how to spot sexual abuse, how to prevent it, and how to respond when they find it. It's real and it happens in the church. BUT, that's no excuse for withholding hugs and care for all children in your ministry. We've become so paranoid that we're afraid to touch kids. The answer is to have a plan in place and follow it.[10]

The BOTTOM LINE is that children need to know love as soon as they are born. Children need to know that what they are sensing in those early years is the presence of God (Jesus) in them—and it's good because God loves them, even more than we do.

Helpful Tips

1. Use all life-passage events, such as baptisms, retreats, parties, etc., as a teaching time to affirm families and encourage the faith community in its people care.
2. Train adults in basic, respectful behavior toward children (e.g. kneeling to the child's height when talking with them, not interrupting a child-adult conversation, not forcing a hug or physical touch, etc.).

---

9   Two great resources on the spiritual development of children: *Joining Children on the Spiritual Journey: Nurturing a Life of Faith* by Catherine Stonehouse (Grand Rapids: Baker Academic, 1998); *Children Matter: Celebrating their Place in the Church, Family and Community* by Beth Posterski, Linda Cannell, Catherine Stonehouse, and Scottie May (Grand Rapids: Eerdmans, 2005).

10 Check out "Reducing the Risk II: Making Your Church Safe From Child Sexual Abuse" at: fmcusa.org/resource/.

3. Guide children to act respectfully toward one another, to choose *helpful* words when talking together; to pray and care for one another as persons carefully created by God in God's image.
4. Create parent-children events that offer experiences for both to learn healthy relationship skills.
5. Train children's workers (teachers) to see themselves, first and foremost, as Village Group leaders of children. They will learn to provide pastoral nurture to the children and their families before, during, and after the time they spend instructing.

WITH TEENS

Think of teens as blossoming young adults. They are not children and if given the opportunity will take responsibility for much of their own lives.

Promote teens out of adolescence.

Adolescence is a creation of our Western advertising culture,[11] and a stage of life that is promoted to all ages—even to senior adults. However, it is possible to help our teens learn to function successfully as young adults. If anyone should take leadership in helping teens break free from the wild culture of adolescence, it's Jesus-followers.

One immediate step is to change our vocabulary from talking about kids or children when relating to teens. Try on the words *young adult* and note the difference.

From our years of trailcamping[12] in Eastern Kentucky we now have generations of adults on record, who were transformed from young teens to young adults in the matter of a short week. We watched teens who came to the trail pregnant, leave as mothers to take responsibility for their babies. We saw macho males, who came "strutting their stuff," return home to live as virginal role models in their high schools—and amaze their parents. We cheered as teenagers came off

---

11 For a more complete discussion (and solutions) for moving teens into adulthood checkout *Empower Your Kids—To Be Adults: A Guide for Parents, Ministers, and Other Mentors* by Donald M. Joy (Nappanee, IN: Evangel Publishing House, 2000, 1-800-253-9315).

12 For many years Discipleship Development Through Trailcamping was an annual class of Asbury Theological Seminary—Kentucky. It included a strenuous week-long wilderness hike with seminarians as staff leaders and high-schoolers as campers.

the trail as seriously committed, young-adult disciples of Jesus.

Great youth ministries will guide teens out of adolescence into vital young adulthood.

Create Relationship Labs

Actually, you may not need to invent new events. Intentionally re-creating healthy-relationship interactions as part of regularly scheduled events may be most effective. Use gaming, small communities, role plays, etc., to put teens into relational practice, where despite cultural or parental expectations, there is no need for pairing off until late teen years.

In addition, modeling mutual respect is vital. As individuals who are carefully designed by God's hand, in God's image, we treat teens and other staff persons with deep respect. And in turn teens learn to treat one another and staff persons with that same respect.

Certainly, there will be times when direct teaching is a must. You will need to describe what respectful behavior looks like and how it gets played out in relationships. And there will also be those times for loving corrective action.

Life-long, Not Instant Sex

Just saying "No" never changes behavior. While it is important for teens to discover God's plan for sex, understanding marriage as a life-long commitment puts a proper framework around discussions of sexuality. And since "I'm going to spend the rest of my life with another person, I would never disrespect someone else's (or my) future spouse by becoming sexually involved outside of that permanent relationship."

Teens at Risk

Parental absence (usually by fathers) is pervasive and devastating. As teens move into puberty, they need a person of the opposite gender (preferably a parent) actively interacting with them; affirming their deep value as humans. Teens without an opposite-gender parent are at the greatest risk of slipping into distorted behavior. Often teen staff members become surrogate parents for teens at risk.

Certainly there are perils in teen-staff interaction if staff adults are not safe people, unable to keep healthy boundaries. Yet, by using both male and female teen leaders, the team can work together, to hold one another accountable.

Young men without *mother-approval*, that affirms and guides males to treat females with respect, tend to become predators and "users" of females. Young women without *father-approval* tend toward promiscuity—looking for any man's approval.

If young women don't have a father to love them, they may try to get pregnant by a man. If the man won't marry them, they may hope to have a male child who will love them. None of this is usually thought through. It is a deep subconscious longing for approval.[13]

Connect grandparent-types

Whether formal relationships are formed or whether you work healthy older adults into your already existing teen events, teens gain the most spiritually from grandparents. Grandparents, one generation older than the teens' parents, can become life models with whom to share life's struggles.

WITH POST-TEEN YOUNG ADULTS

Most young adults are more or less in active pursuit of a life-long partner, whether or not they are willing to make the needed commitment—or say so out loud. Each person experiences a "universal longing for an exclusive, permanent marriage from childhood to death." As male and female, God created us with an "internal reminder"—a "magnetic attention"—to seek an alternative to our aloneness.[14] Thus, young adults may respond with greater interest when considering the growth of healthy relationships, leading to a life partner.

However, with the increasing age of first marriage, you would never want to assume that all young adults are ready to take the marriage leap. This means that when discussing relationships or providing opportunities for relationship growth, both singleness and *coupleness* need to be included. Singles need to know how to survive (finding

---

13 For a thorough discussion of family systems and the spin-offs of various models, see *Risk-Proofing Your Family* by Donald M. Joy, US Center for World Mission, 1995, Phone 800-647-7466 (www.donaldjoy.com).

14 In discussion with Dr. Donald Joy, June 23, 2009.

fulfillment and wholeness) in the in-between years that may last a lifetime.

It is essential to create specific events, usually retreat-type weekends, for couples to explore their future together. I know one church that offers annual relationship weekends (for those not yet dating or who are just beginning to date), pre-engaged weekends (for seriously-dating couples), and Engaged Encounter (for those moving quickly toward the marriage altar).[15]

The Village Group may provide the safe haven of intimate relationships that postpones marriage and affirms a young adult's singleness.

Despite your communication skill, it is often best to bring in an outside resource person to say what you want said to your post-teen adults. Using an intense community setting [such as a three-night (minimum) retreat or an adventure ministry] can quickly produce a life-lab that you could only hope to experience in a year or more. In a life-lab you will see amazing changes and growth if you're prepared to deal with the issues that arise.

Cheer for the Singles

A faith community must be a safe place for those who are not yet married, are no longer married, or will never marry.

Yet so often it's not.

Singles are created in the same image of God as those who marry. They are not somehow "half-bearers" of the image of God. And healthy relationships with the opposite gender are not only possible but important to both the community of faith and to singles—especially single parents for whom we carry a great responsibility!

Volumes of research have proved the incredible impact of single-parenting on both the parent and the children. There is not room to cover it in detail here. Suffice it to say, as a faith community we are to surround single-parent families with support and special care; to provide surrogate parents for the children; to help carry the burden of the single-parent in every way possible. It truly takes a village to raise a family.

---

15 Wooddale Church in Minneapolis, MN, has created an amazing model, and has shared their vision most generously. Check out www.wooddale.org.

As Jesus-followers we *will* affirm singles in their singleness, through our careful care, whether or not they ever marry.

WITH MIDDLE AND OLDER ADULTS

At no time can we stop caring for healthy relationships, both generally, and in marriages specifically. Most of us know the stories of church fights where "good Christians who just can't get along," end up in a church split over the bathroom paint color. The same is true for marriages. We know the tragedy of the *perfect* couple who announce to their friends that they're breaking up after 10 or 20 years of marriage.

As Christians we're always on a relationship-rescue mission with one another.

The first year of marriage

Research points to the fact that first-year-marriage-care is vital for marriage survival. As we'll discuss in a later chapter, you will want a Mentor Couple to nurture each engaged couple through the last six months of engagement and through the first year of marriage.

Life-stressors

You can make your own list, but we know that early marriages need special care surrounding them. So do marriages that start after 30 years of age, particularly when children arrive about the third anniversary. Career changes and retirement, especially for men who so strongly attach personal value to a job, can cause relationships to hit the rocks. Then there are those times when illness, catastrophic injury or death (particularly that of a child in the family) shock a person or family to their spiritual and emotional roots. All are intense life-stressors where the faith community must be alert to help.

Blended families

Even more difficult than bringing two lives together in a first marriage is merging two families. Trying to create health out of what is often relationship chaos takes great patience and intense care. The survival of blended families is usually precarious at best.

Un-retire grandparents

As mentioned earlier, seniors are usually the best, untapped resource in any congregational setting. Some feel burned out and will take a little (or a lot of) persuading. Others feel bored or unneeded and will jump at the chance to help with younger folk. Seniors bring experience—sometimes with only a little coaching—and wisdom to relationships. Remember, grandparents usually have a greater spiritual impact than anyone else you can place with your children, youth or young adults.

Teach about biblical relationships

Sermons are not times for editorializing our favorite hot topic. However, we can use those moments, particularly with biblical stories (since Mary and Joseph may be the only ones who got it right, after an un-wed pregnancy) to demonstrate real-life struggles and godly principles for relationships. The Sermon on the Mount (Matthew 5–7) is a good place to find a year's worth of sermons.[16]

When teaching or preaching on marriage and relationships, tell the truth. Much of what we read about relationships is pure fabrication. Avoid presenting "truth" from blogs (often just shared ignorance and gossip). If you cannot support a point from a reliable source, do not present it as fact. Christians have a well-deserved reputation for jumping on a gossip campaign, ending up looking foolish at best or really nasty at worst. When you do feel the need to share a serious truth, remember to share it *positively*—teach what God has to say that would redeem a difficult statistic (e.g. the number of couples who cohabitate). Remember our job is to offer Good News, not condemnation.

Stories are the most powerful tool that God has given us. Our sermons/teachings should be filled with them. We have God's story through history—written in the Bible and lived through the ages of the church. We have the *other person's* story. Use interviews (live or on video) to let people share what God has done in their lives. We have *our story*. Live and share your life transparently (both the successes and failures)—even as part of the sermon. When those three stories connect, the Holy Spirit does powerful work.

16 Let Jesus do the talking. Check out our team's *Radical Journey* at www.Lulu.com. It's a 20-week immersion with Jesus in the Sermon on the Mount; including individual study, Village Group sessions, and missional experiences.

Offer Crisis Care

As mentioned earlier, you can never create a ministry for every need that arises in your faith community. You will want to choose the two or three areas that match the needs of your congregation or community, and where you have qualified persons who are passionate about the need, and volunteer to lead.[17] However, as you start adding new Village Groups, start by targeting specific needs.

One important ministry for you to partner with is Retrouvaille.[18] It is the most effective ministry for bringing recovery to troubled or broken marriages. It is similar to Marriage Encounter[19] except that Retrouvaille is facilitated by people who have lived through relational brokenness and successfully come out on the other side.

IF a couple is willing to take one more chance toward reconciliation, they should attend a Retrouvaille weekend retreat. Following the first weekend event are seven follow-up weeks where couples report back their progress on each week's assignments.

Offer Marriage Boosters

Premarital preparation doesn't last a lifetime. It has been found effective for about the first eight years of marriage, then declines as family circumstances change.

Marriage Encounter provides a great marriage boost. You may also connect to one of the other couple-events that are marketed across the country. Just make sure that what is taught about couple relationships is truly biblical; not based on some sort of male-hierarchical model.

Another option is to search out resource people and create your own "weekend away" where couples who are acquainted with one another can share relaxed time with both their spouses and the larger group. Upon returning home, they will have a commonality that could become the foundation for a small community or future *check-ups*.

17 Based on my own failures, I tell people to never start a new ministry with a solo leader. NEVER! All ministries must be led by teams—a minimum of two. Think Village Group/ Team.

18 You can find out more from www.retrouvaille.org. Look for retreat weekends in your area.

19 See World Wide Marriage Encounter at www.wwme.org. Several denominations have their own version of the Encounter. You may visit the Mennonites and Brethren at www.marriage-encounter.org.

Members of this group can function to hold one another accountable for keeping their marriages healthy.

AGAIN, IT'S THE AIR WE BREATHE

The pervasive atmosphere that people experience in our faith communities should be healthy relationships with God and one another. The core of our ministries must center on small communities (Village Groups), where those healthy relationships are tested and lived out— touching the lives of those outside the church walls. That relational and community health will grow people who come to marriage with the best advantages for life-long success.

4

Opportunities

Weddings and marriage ministry may force us into some of the most controversial issues faced by a faith community. They also will give us opportunity to serve those whom others will ignore or even reject.

As you remember, Jesus patterned for us by touching those considered outcasts, those who were different, and pronouncing wholeness.

You'll also remember that his behavior crazed those conservatives, the Pharisees, who called Jesus a liberal (glutton, drunkard)[1] because he broke the rules, hanging out with the wrong crowd. And the liberal zealots who couldn't entice him into a battle for independence from Rome betrayed him. Both—conspiring together—killed him.

He was a RADICAL—meaning deeply rooted. Radicals are rooted deeply in God's Kingdom values and refuse to let anyone put them into a labeled box. But it's a risky way to live.

Any time we attempt to create healthy relationships in a community, varying life scenarios will surface. It seems to me that we have two choices.

One, we can write off the people who admit they struggle or who live differently than us, and exclude them from our community.

Two, we can admit we all struggle at some level—no more pretending—and seek to care for each person in whatever life situation they find themselves.

---

1 See Matthew 11:19 and Luke 7:34 as examples.

I'm assuming that you're choosing number two or you'll close the book at this point. If you're available for serving all people, great opportunities await.

AIM POSITIVELY

All that said, when we look at marriages and families we can easily become overwhelmed. It's a choice to live expectantly—to think positively.

For example, you've probably heard many times that 50% of all marriages end in divorce, that most couples live together before marriage, that abortion and teenage pregnancy are on the increase, that most teens are sexually active, and that the institution of marriage is "on the rocks." And that's just for starters.

Only one of those assumptions is actually true.

So before you get depressed, let me encourage you to consider what it would mean if we looked for positive opportunities to minister to those whom others will reject.

First though, let's look at a potential trap.

AVOID THE TRAP

We can easily fall into the assumption that complex issues have simple "yes" and "no" answers. That's a sad hangover from our declining modernistic philosophy and too much Fox News. Most of us realize there are no simple answers to complex issues of life.

As Jesus followers we must always add an "AND." In God's Kingdom we must often hold onto two, seemingly opposing, views at the same time. The "AND" looks at peoples' real-life situations.

If you've studied statistics you know this is true.

Everything depends on how we interpret the statistics and what point we are trying to make. Unfortunately, several family issues have become so politicized that we cannot discuss them with any sort of rational or biblical integrity.

May I speak frankly as a pastor? Let's stop throwing barbs at one another, inside and outside the faith community. Much of what we espouse as truth is simply urban legend: simply nonsense! Most of our beliefs about marriage, divorce and relationships are so ingrained that they have become part of our faith-community fabric, whether true or not. Yet we fail to offer our culture a grace-filled message of hope.

But don't get me wrong. Careful research is important.

We must not remain ignorant if we have the opportunity to gain insight. And none of us has the time to dig through all the available data, sort it for ourselves, make sense of it, and share it. So, we must cautiously depend on others to help us sort through the reams of valid research that exists along with the myths.

But recognize that every researcher comes to work with their own biases and theological bents. And since no one can separate themselves from their deep-seated beliefs, their data will tend to give the answers they are looking for. It's then our responsibility to honestly evaluate the available evidence and commit ourselves to bringing healing instead of making theological or political points.

Avoiding this ministry trap, let's consider a few of the special ministry opportunities all around us.

SPECIAL OPPORTUNITIES

Watch for Couple Care (or lack thereof)

John Gottman and Robert Levenson[2] found two key factors that seem to predict divorce with 93% accuracy. Their research focused on both the presence of "negative affect" (their word for issues like contempt, criticism, defensiveness and stonewalling) and the absence of "positive affect" (their word for issues like affection, interest and humor).

While common sense would point toward high levels of conflict as destroying a relationship, they found that the absence of positive affect is just as deadly for a long-term marriage.

> The major reasons for divorce, cited by nearly 80% of all men and women, was gradually growing apart and losing a sense of close-ness and not feeling loved and appreciated....Thus, it could be the case that marriages characterized by intense fighting dissolve soon-er than do those characterized as without positive affect....People may stay together but become emotionally detached, postponing

2 Gottman, John Mordechai and Levenson, Robert Wayne, "The Timing of Divorce: Predicting When a Couple Will Divorce Over a 14-Year Period," *Journal of Marriage and the Family* 62, (August 2000); 737-745.

divorce until their loneliness becomes unbearable and the need to remain married (e.g. to raise children) becomes less compelling.[3]

So as leaders we need to be alert to relational drift among our longer married couples; those whom we'd never anticipate experiencing relational difficulty since they appear to have lived as successful marrieds for numerous years.

Watch for Spiritual Compatibility

Many studies point toward the possibility for more healthy couple relationships, if couples are religiously compatible. However, most studies fail to look at the deeper issues of faith and couple compatibility. Most are too narrow in their scope and incorrectly defining *religious*.

They use a single factor such as frequency of church attendance or shared church affiliation as the *religious indicator*. They measure religious *activity* instead of *belief and values*.

In addition, several studies show that when evangelical couples are compared to other couples, the divorce rate is the same. Something is missing. Religious life and belief can be either a point of deep compatibility or a source of deep division.

In a large study from the PREPARE/ENRICH program, Olson and Olson discovered that a key factor in couple happiness was "how spiritual values and beliefs were expressed."[4] In other words, not only consensus on spiritual practices but also on spiritual beliefs leads to more positive marital functioning. In fact, "higher couple consensus on spiritual beliefs was associated with higher couple agreement on every other ENRICH scale."[5]

Spiritual beliefs (more than religious practice) impact all the other areas of married life. Couples who experienced consensus on spiritual issues were strongly committed to egalitarian roles and scored high on the other "closeness scales" (Personality Issues, Communication, Con-

---

3 Ibid., page 738.

4 Olson, D.H. & Olson, A.K., *Empowering Couples: Building on Your Strengths* (Minneapolis: Life Innovations, Inc., 2000) in Larson, Peter J. & Olson, David H., "Spiritual Beliefs and Marriage: A National Survey Based on ENRICH," an unpublished article (Minneapolis: Life Innovations, Inc., cir. 2003), p. 3–4.

5 Olson, D.H. & Olson, A.K., 7.

flict Resolution and Sexual Relationship).[6] They also had the lowest risk of divorce among the five types of couples that ENRICH studies.

Watch for the Big Three

While there are many issues to discuss when guiding a couple toward marriage, three factors always float to the top as primary conflict triggers in the earliest years of a marriage: balancing job and family (time), frequency of sexual relations (sex), and financial issues (money).[7]

While most couples list the BIG THREE as the greatest issues they face early in marriage, the truth may be that these factors precipitate difficulty in other couple issues like communication and healthy conflict resolution.

In a culture where both spouses usually work, it is predictable that balancing work and family would cause concern.

The same is true for frequency of sexual relations. Sometimes the issue is time availability for intimacy. Sometimes the issue is learning each other's sexual needs and language. Couples with children have an even higher level of frustration with the lack of sexual involvement since intimate time is more difficult to find. When work is factored in, the difficulty is even more pronounced.

Then we add the third factor—money. Financial issues take many forms from past debt to school bills, from spending beyond income levels to lack of emergency savings, from disagreements about living style to levels of charitable giving. Whatever the case, it adds up to a flashpoint.

We can easily imagine an explosive situation when couples work too many hours, spend too little time with one another, communicate ineffectively, neglect time for sexual intimacy, and are dealing with financial stress.

While newly married couples, particularly those over 30 years old, may appear to have a handle on life, it's usually not true. They have lived long enough on their own to create patterns of living that do not include one another. Everything from how they unroll the toilet paper

6   Larson, P. J. & Olson, D. H., "Spiritual Beliefs and Marriage: A National Survey Based on ENRICH," a non-published article. (Spring 2004), 1–14.

7   Risch, Gail. S., Riley, Lisa. A. & Lawler, Michael G., "Problematic Issues in the Early Years of Marriage: Content for Premarital Education," *Journal of Psychology and Theology*, Rosemead School of Psychology Biola University (2003).

to how they squeeze the toothpaste tube has become ingrained in their personal practices. Now when they combine two *in-place* lives, relationships can fracture. Often they continue to live as married-singles, treating one another as intruders into their own private world.

As touched on earlier, the most vulnerable time for couples who marry after 30 years of age is when they give birth to their first child. We as ministry leaders must be assertive enough to step into those relationships, to let those couples know we care and we will not let them break up easily, nor alone.

When we focus on the three trigger factors, we can help couples discover tools for dealing with these stressors as they come. We will watch for couples who are living through the three-to-five-year window of marriage, for signs of sickness; being especially vigilant to those who are 30 years of age or older, and who have just birthed a child. They are living in a "distressed range."[8]

Watch for Cohabitating Couples

Far too much judgment has been poured onto couples who *practice marriage* in an uncommitted live-in relationship. Yet there is no easy answer to why couples cohabitate. For some, it's simply for monogamous sex without the commitment of marriage. For others, it involves a deep commitment to a relationship and a simultaneous deep fear of marriage. And for others, cohabitating is primarily an economic decision. Communal living is less expensive.

Should we be surprised when young people, who have grown up watching their parents stomp on their own marriage vows—passing children back and forth like another piece of furniture—want to try out this thing called marriage before doing it for real? Or why would they ever make a marriage commitment when so many assume it will never last anyway? And when we look at our role models—the rich and famous—unmarried family life seems to work successfully, at least for a time.

Yet, in a culture of short-term commitments—or none at all—we have the opportunity to offer a voice of hope and a future.

---

8 Risch, Gail. S., Riley, Lisa. A. & Lawler, Michael G. "Problematic Issues in the Early Years of Marriage."

Cohabitation vs. Marriage

The dangers of cohabitation are well documented.

In one study, at least 40% of cohabitating couples break up before marriage. Of those who married, 75% ended in divorce. In other words, out of 100 cohabitating couples, 40 break up before marriage. Of the 60 who marry, 45 will divorce within 10 years. That leaves only 15 couples intact after 10 years.[9]

Cohabitating unions tend to weaken the institution of marriage and pose special risks for women and children. For example:

Living together before marriage **increases the risk of breaking up after marriage.**

Living together outside of marriage **increases the risk of domestic violence for women**, and **the risk of physical and sexual abuse among children.**

Unmarried couples have **lower levels of happiness and wellbeing** than married couples.[10]

While there is some disagreement as to whether cohabitation itself is the cause for increased divorce, most researchers agree that the level of education, spiritual faith, level of income, and family background are key factors in who cohabitates and whose marriages break up.

We do know that cohabitation is higher among women who have dropped out of high school versus those who have graduated from college.

Cohabitation is also more common among those who are less religious than their peers, those who have been divorced, and those who have experienced parental divorce, fatherlessness, or high levels of marital discord during childhood. And a growing percentage of cohabiting couple households, now over 40 percent, contain children.[11]

Yes, cohabitation is a serious issue and appears to be increasing at all religious, socio-economic, and educational levels. But, I grieve

---

9   McManus, Mike, "Marriage Savers Answers 25 Tough Questions," an on-line publication at www.marriagesavers.com/public/marriage_savers_answers_25_tough.htm (2004) (Marriage Savers, 9311 Harrington Drive, Potomac, MD 20854), 2.

10 "Should We Live Together?" by David Popenoe and Barbara Dafoe Whitehead, The National Marriage Project, Rutgers, The State University of New Jersey (2002), 1.

11 "The State of Our Unions 2007: The Social Health of Marriage in America," The National Marriage Project, Rutgers, The State University of New Jersey (July 2007), 20.

most for those who break up, who've already experienced the pain of divorce before knowing the joy of marriage.

Missing Divorce

The accurate data show that the divorce rate is declining—probably down to about 33–35%. Though that sounds like good news, it points to the fact that fewer couples are getting married, instead choosing cohabitation. "It is estimated that about a quarter of unmarried women age 25 to 39 are currently living with a partner and an additional quarter have lived with a partner at some time in the past. Over half of all first marriages are now preceded by living together, compared to virtually none 50 years ago."[12]

No matter how agonizing a divorce, divorced couples know when the proceedings are final. They walk out of the courtroom with a document that brings a bit of closure to the failed marriage. When cohabitating couples separate, they miss the benefit of a divorce. They walk away with fragments of a mangled relationship. They tend to pick up their pillow, their clothes, a few towels and move on.

And they carry the shreds of that brokenness into their next relationship; usually never dealing with all the stuff they're dragging behind.

Think of it this way. When a couple is divorced, the closure papers are something like cauterizing a bleeding wound. The scar remains but much of the bleeding stops. When cohabitating couples breakup, it's like pulling a wound in two, leaving the open vessels to continue bleeding—then attaching to another relationship and the tragedy continues.

While the analogy is not perfect, it points to the fact that though the divorce figures are down, the number of broken, pain-filled relationships is on the increase and millions of persons carry deep trauma.

The implications of cohabitation are gigantic. But there are ways to reduce the cohabitation rate, to help couples catch a dream of God's best plan for them, to bring God's restorative presence to those who have already cohabitated. And we have the honor of partnering with the Creator in this work.

---

12 That totals over 50% of all women 25–39 years of age. "The State of Our Unions 2007: The Social Health of Marriage in America," 19.

Cohabitating Couples at Your Door

Whatever the reasons for cohabitation, you and I must decide how we'll work with couples who now desire marriage after cohabitation. Part of the importance for an extensive pre- and post-marital plan, is to dig under the surface, to discover what's driving the decision for a couple to move from cohabitation to marriage. Too often the decision to wed comes out of a painful crisis in living together; the couple believing that marriage will solve the problem. Yet, those who marry to solve a crisis nearly always end up in divorce.

Should We Break Them Up?

Some ministry leaders force cohabitating couples into celibacy during the engagement. However, as Jesus-followers, we must not violate the Creation principle of "not separating what God had joined together"—damaging the sacred bond between them.[13] The creation bond is already in place, with or without the formal ceremony.

Our role is to protect that bond.

In addition, we would never want to force couples to lie about their involvement or magnify the guilt they carry by invading their private sexual world.

The best option for cohabitating couples might be to follow the example of Mary and Joseph. Pregnant with Jesus, they were never married in a traditional extravagant wedding. With family and close friends surrounding, we can sanctify the bond that God is creating with a simple wedding and reception.

Paint a Dream

Rather than *requiring* a cohabitating couple to stop sexual activity during engagement, we can paint a dream for them. We can *challenge them to choose* to stop sexual activity for the specific purpose of using the engagement as a period of deep growth with God, a time for richer relational growth with one another, and a fresh beginning for their life-long commitment. The honeymoon then becomes a glorious place where two newly-minted virgins meet, rather than just another vacation together.[14]

---

13 See Matthew 19:6, Mark 10:9. This is a difficult discussion and different counselors have varying opinions of what is most healthy for the couple's long-term relationship.

14 See Paul's admonition in 1 Corinthians 7:5 describing the need for a mutual decision.

From my experience, we've generally had good results when co-habiting couples decide to remain sexually celibate during engagement. It's never easy once intimacy has been shared, but it can be done. Often the couple has misunderstood the deeper issues involved in living together. They've seen couples living together in the media, who exude "happiness ever after," or their friends pressured them to move in together as the next step in serious dating. When the couple understands that they can start over, that the honeymoon can be a new beginning, they often jump at the chance.

Certainly some couples don't see a way to live separately if they are dependent upon one another financially. That makes celibacy even more difficult.

Most importantly, we must remain committed to working with each couple where they are, helping them move closer to God's original plan without laying more judgment upon them.

One final point. We have noticed that cohabiting couples who choose celibacy during engagement may still need special counseling once married, to experience full healing. The ghosts of the past may raise their heads and cause emotional and sexual difficulty. This is also where creating a *Divorce-Care* type of class for formerly cohabiting couples could prove helpful.

Watch for Same-Sex Partnerships

This section is difficult to write since I have colleagues and friends on all sides of the issue. And my views are evolving as I seek God's clarity.

We could argue, as my dad used to say, "until we're blue in the face" but we'd be no closer to discovering why some people prefer intimacy with persons of the same gender—nor its biblical morality. Psychologists to theologians to most blog pages have offered opinions. Various researchers have proposed causes for same-sex preference such as:

childhood sexual abuse,

lack of same-gender bonding by males at puberty,

social pressure,

poor gender models in the family,

personal preference,

or genetics.

And honest, orthodox, Jesus-followers have studied the Bible and come to different conclusions as to what the few biblical verses really mean that we associate with prohibition against homosexuality.

So rather than label our brothers and sisters on the various sides of the issue—or cut ourselves off from them—we must find another way to proceed. Those whom God called to live in unity have already done enough damage to the body of Christ.

Dr. Steve Harper gives us a healthy reminder that the Church's understanding, across the centuries, is that those who ascribe to the historic creeds have been considered orthodox.[15] Differences on other issues are just differences of opinion. And the Church has fractured too many times over differences of opinion.[16]

Of course, knowing that concept doesn't make the issue of same-gender partnerships or marriage simple to discuss.

A Homophobic Church?
The one glaring fact is that the LGBTQ[17] community has mostly been cut off by homophobia from the Christian church.

While my denomination will not allow me to preside over same-sex weddings, it seems justice and grace require me to support some form of legal rights and protection from discrimination for LGBT people. How can I tell my gay and lesbian friends that God loves them—no matter what—and allow for hatred by people who profess faith in Jesus? How can I sit by and allow for discrimination of any persons and still profess to follow Jesus?

Not possible!

Since all states must allow for same-sex marriage, whatever our personal views (or those of our ministry groups), if we're going to be instruments of God's love, we must learn to live with humility and confession for our corporate hate toward LGBT people.

So, how do I as a pastor, committed to the creation story of the

---

15 Think *Apostles' Creed* and *Nicene Creed*. Check out Justin S. Holcomb's *Know the Heretics* (from the KNOW Series) (Grand Rapids: Zondervan, 2014).

16 Dr. Steve Harper is the founding Vice President of Asbury Seminary—FL Dunnam Campus, retired spiritual formation professor, pastor, biblical scholar, and prolific author.

17 LGBT, an acronym for lesbian, gay, bi-sexual, transgender individuals. Often LGBT people add Q for *queer* ... not as a derogatory term, but instead as a more encompassing expression for all gay people.

first man and first woman, respond to a same-gender relationship? How do I model Jesus, who specifically sought out the outcasts? What do I say to committed Jesus-followers living in a same-sex relationship? How do I live out Jesus' command to respect and protect the bond between two people who are faithfully committed to one another?

Live Love

I have no simple answers—maybe no answers. I just know that I must be prepared to serve those who come to us, and never turn anyone away without speaking grace into their lives.

In other words, the Great Commandments of loving God and loving my neighbor as myself must take on skin through me.

While we will not all agree we can spend time in careful, respectful discussion with LGBTQ people; getting to truly know and love them, and their needs.[18] And we must continue praying and searching the Scriptures; reconsidering whether our interpretations of a few difficult passages come from tradition, our biases, or honest searching. Over the centuries the Church has too often taught what was espoused as biblical when in reality the ideas were out of context or misinterpretations. And millions have suffered.

Let's not do that again.

Most of all, we must live into the full understanding that God's Spirit will always compel us to serve and love all persons or groups who come our way.

WHAT NOW?

With so much at stake, how do we sort out the multitude of special ministry opportunities? Where can we start to make difference? Shall we work to repair damaged relationships or shall we work to help persons start healthy? Obviously the answer is "Yes" to both.

But that mission seems overwhelming. So, as you meditate on this chapter, begin to dream God's dream for your Marriage/relational Ministry.

---

18 Get a copy of *For the Sake of the Bride: Restoring the Church to Her Intended Beauty,* 2nd edition by Steve Harper (Abingdon, 2014). He gives us a way to work through difficult and divisive issues with respect for those we disagree with, while keeping the unity that Jesus prayed for his body in John 15–17.

Dream the big *WHAT IFs*. Then pick one or two ways that you can faithfully respond to the need.

Remember, any dream big enough to be God's dream is big enough that you cannot accomplish it alone or without God's help. That's when it gets exciting!

5

Setting the Stage

It was the second wedding I had performed for the grandchild of
a couple in my congregation. We'd completed minimal premarital
preparation. I just knew that the grandma wanted her granddaughter
married in our sanctuary with the 50-foot stained glass window.

Neither the bride nor the groom professed a story of Christian
faith. They just wanted the wedding done as soon as possible and
agreed to allow me to talk about Jesus in their ceremony.

Two weeks before the big day I realized that we should not be
performing the wedding. Something was missing but I couldn't put my
finger on it. I just sensed they were not ready for marriage, now. Probably they should never marry each other.

So, I had several choices.

Would I offend the grandparents by refusing to perform the wedding? Would I try to convince the couple to delay their wedding while
we did additional work? Would I just go ahead and please everyone,
performing the wedding as if I saw no issues?

That was the last wedding I performed until we created a plan to
give couples a fighting chance for surviving a life-long marriage.

This chapter lays out a simple plan that works. It's a model that
can be adapted—because we've done it—in all sizes and types of congregations. The key is—be intentional in developing a plan.

But let's not get ahead ourselves. Before you can create a plan, your
faith community will need to make some principled decisions on some
difficult issues.

SET WEDDING CRITERIA AND HOLD TO THEM

It is important for congregations to set guidelines for engaged couples, whether or not a grandparent is a long-time member of your church. And the criteria must be published with buy-in from all congregational leadership.

While the criteria should be firm, they must be principle-based, having enough flexibility to be adaptable for specific situations. For example, if you say that all couples must have six months of premarital preparation with your ministry before the wedding, that's great. However, if a couple comes to you who've been working through counseling in another agency, you will want to evaluate what they have experienced and create an adapted model for them—combining what they've already completed with what you want them to complete with you.

Don't fear being firm. The couple's future is at stake whether they know it or not. They will thank you later.

Here are **FIVE** key questions to consider as you begin creating your guidelines.

- *Do we marry cohabitating couples if they are still living together?*
  We've already discussed many of the issues. But since approximately 60% of the couples who come to you for a wedding ceremony will be living together, and most of those have no biblical or church background, there may be better a question to ask: "Who will minister to the needs of this couple if you choose not to?"

  The answer to that question is never easy. Just sure make that the grace of Jesus is your guiding principle.
- *How many months of pre-marital counseling must a couple complete before the wedding?*
  In the next chapter we'll give a plan that includes six months of premarital work and one year post-marital work. That should be a minimum, including meeting with a Mentor Couple[1] at least six times.
- *Must the bride and groom be members of your congregation or will you do weddings for "all comers"?*

---

1   The plan for Mentor Couples is introduced in a few pages.

Do you see your ministry site as a wedding rent-a-chapel? Do you have plans for life-long follow up with couples whom you marry? Are weddings of non-connected people part of your ministry strategy?

Don't respond to this question by default. Make a *missional decision*. The first pastor who mentored me grew a congregation by performing weddings for anyone who asked—those rejected by other pastors. These *unwanted* couples became his ministry target, and he led most to Jesus, over time.

➤ *Will you marry only Christians to Christians?*
Certainly there is a biblical mandate for being "equally yoked" together. Could the premarital work be a chance for evangelism? Do you have a pastor or Mentor Couple with the gift of evangelism? Do you have sensitive ways to help couples delay their weddings—or cancel altogether?

➤ *Will you marry or bless same-sex couples?*
As we've discussed previously, if the laws in your state allow for same-sex marriage, you will need to decide whether your congregation will perform them or leave those weddings for the state. Will you be a voice for Jesus-care in the lives of LGBT persons? If so, how?

One denomination does not allow their pastors to perform same-sex weddings but does allow clergy to participate in the wedding by doing something like reading scripture. That's something to consider.

These are difficult, and important, questions you will need to answer. You'll probably have your own long list of other issues to consider as well. Denominational leaders will make some decisions for you. Others you'll answer at a congregational level. However, you'll need consensus as a leadership team and governing board on what to enforce. All leaders become targets for their friends who will try to bypass the guidelines for their own whims. However, remember to work from a position of "firm grace"—committed to life-long marriages—and not a legalistic list of rules.

A WORD OF ENCOURAGEMENT

Taking the time to get it "right" with couples is critical for life-long marriages. But you cannot create a marriage ministry by yourself. Whether you're a pastor or a leader in the congregation—think *team*. You and your congregation can create a plan to make it happen—but only if you do it together. The goal is to STOP just *doing weddings* and become a *marriage-safe ministry*. Of course, a pastor will usually preside over weddings, but weddings won't be an end in themselves. Weddings will become a great, public worship celebration for the beginning of a life-long marriage.

A WORD OF WARNING

If you didn't already know it, weddings are a hot topic. When you start implementing a structured plan for Marriage Ministry, you may face fierce opposition. Despite how many times we decry the divorce rate, when it comes to making a change in how we do weddings the fur can hit the fan.

When I first introduced our *new* marriage ministry plan to one congregation, the people I expected to support it most heartily were the ones who challenged me the most. They said, "Why are you making it so hard for our kids to get married? My granddaughter...."

However, after many explanations,[2] holding firm to what we believed would work, and watching results appear, overwhelming support evolved for what we did.

One couple, in their mid-thirties and heading into their first marriage, shared with me during one of our sessions together. They said, "We've been telling our friends what we're working through in preparation for our marriage. They are amazed. They wonder how we could know so much about marriage before our wedding; things they are just discovering after 10 years of marriage."

---

2 We affirmed that we loved their grandchildren too. And since we loved them so much, we were doing all we could to assure that the marriages we performed would last a lifetime.

GETTING THE RIGHT PEOPLE IN PLACE

Rudy and Faith Buettner[3] challenged me to create a plan that would make a difference for our engaged couples—to stop acting as a rent-a-pastor at a wedding chapel.

After searching for models from which to borrow, we found Wooddale Church in Minneapolis, MN[4]—a vital congregation that is committed to life-long marriages. They encouraged us, and let us borrow and adapt at will. From everything we learned, we changed, we grew, and we added new ideas to create our own model. You can do the same in your context.

We suggest that a marriage ministry team have at least four people: a Pastor,
a Mentor Couple,
and a Wedding Coordinator.

Very soon you will want to add a Coordinator/Director (choose your own title) of Marriage Ministry. This person (preferably a couple) will lead and grow the ministry team, and carry out your vision.

The Pastor

The lead pastor of a congregation must be the primary advocate for healthy relationships in general and the specific processes for marriage preparation. No matter how respected an associate pastor or congregational leader is, if they propose an idea that is not totally endorsed by the ministry leader, the plan will never get off the ground.

If you are a lead (solo) pastor, you may need to take the initial administrative role of creating a Marriage Ministry model and putting the team together. This should never be seen as a continuing role. Once a team is in place, let them fly with a Marriage Ministry Director. The pastor must step back, conducting only periodic check-ins to confirm that the vision flame is still burning, and to encourage the Director.

---

3 Rudy and Faith Buettner (Rudy has passed away), as retired volunteers, created an Engaged Encounter weekend, continuously pushed us until we got serious about couple care, became our Marriage Ministry Coordinators, and Mentor Couple trainers. They believed that if their marriage could survive the crisis they faced many years earlier, every marriage should survive—or at least deserved a fighting chance.
4 Check out Wooddale Church (http://wooddale.org/about/you/weddings).

For legal and official church purposes, a pastor[5] must usually perform the central part of the wedding worship. On a pastoral team, the designated pastor becomes the lead pastor for a particular wedding whether or not that is her/his title on the ministry team. She or he will create the wedding worship with the engaged couple, give pastoral guidance (in probably two or three sessions) to the engaged couple, and oversee the worship event on the wedding day. However, most *marriage preparation* should be done with the Mentor Couple. *Wedding preparation* is worked out with the Wedding Coordinator.

As pastors we tend to think we're effective in preparing couples for marriage. But numerous studies show that couples who are counseled only by clergy have a much lower rate of marriage success than when the pastor and a Mentor Couple partner together.

If you create or send engaged couples to an engaged weekend, you'll increase their chance of marriage success even more.

> "A team approach is best, meeting with the clergy...
> in combination with a weekend retreat led by married
> couples [e.g. Engaged Encounter] and meeting with married couples [the Mentor Couple] on a one-on-one basis
> appears to be an ideal way to structure marriage preparation in a church setting."[6]

The Mentor Couple

Marriage researchers agree that the most important piece of preparation for a life-long marriage is connecting an engaged couple to a Mentor Couple. And you want the *right* Mentor Couple(s).

I didn't say the *perfect* couple, since none exist.

5   **Pastor** includes: senior pastor, associate pastor, assistant pastor, or any other title you may use for the person responsible for spiritual oversight of a congregation or group of people.

6   "An Empirical Approach to Designing Marriage Preparation Programs" by Lee Williams, Lisa A. Riley, Gail S. Risch, and David T. Van Dyke, *The American Journal of Family Therapy* (Brunner/Mazel, 1999) 27: 279-280

Often the *right* Mentor Couple has struggled with the deepest heartbreaks but God has turned those broken pieces into a sculpture of grace. Look for people who have experienced the ups and downs of life but seem healthy with one another and with persons of all ages. They may or may not be recognized leaders in your congregation but willingly give themselves as servants to others.

The first step in finding Mentor Couples is for the pastor or Marriage Ministry Coordinator to sit down with prospective mentors, to share the ministry vision and evaluate the couple's interest in giving themselves to engaged couples. As mentors they have the opportunity to imprint a Creation legacy into the life of another couple. While a staff couple may have vital interest in Marriage Ministry, it is best to use non-clergy. Staff persons can be the back-up team, as needed.

Approval of a Mentor Couple should never be done by one person. Make it a team decision of four or five people that includes a pastor or pastors, maybe a pastor's cabinet or board member. The additional people will help to identify if there are issues that should be considered before using a couple as mentors. Once the team decision is made all will support it if there are congregational questions raised.

If a couple is open to signing on as a Mentor Couple they must complete a marriage profile such as REFOCCUS[7] or Enrich[8] to evaluate the quality of their marriage and whether they are dealing with the unavoidable issues in healthy ways. Two topics to carefully check are *finances* and *communication*. Some couples may discover they have too much personal baggage to immediately start as a Mentor Couple, so may delay joining the team. Other couples may need for you to tell them that they are not ready for the team.

Once a couple is approved for service, they must be trained. On-the-job training is most effective. However, your Mentor Couple(s) needs the basics to get started. They must be trained by the agency

7 This is the married couple's version of the premarital *FOCCUS* material from FOCCUS, Inc., 3214 North 60th Street, Omaha, NE 68104; 402.827.3735. You can explore their website at www.foccusinc.com. This group is my favorite since they write from a Christian perspective, out of the Omaha Diocese (the creators of Marriage Encounter, decades ago).

8 This is the married couple's version of the premarital *Prepare* material from Life Innovations, P.O. Box 190, Minneapolis, MN 55440; 800.331.1661. You can explore their website at www. prepare-enrich.com.

that is supplying the profile (e.g. FOCCUS[9] or Life Innovations) you choose for your ministry.

They will continue to receive periodic checkups to improve their skills. The follow-up training should include:

- Discovering the role of a mentor as different from counselor or pastor.
- Using the married couple profile, e.g. *REFOCCUS* or *Enrich*
- Becoming familiar with other referral ministries that can help engaged or married couples with specific needs
- Giving healthy guidance to family budgeting

The Mentor Couple will work with an engaged couple to complete the marriage profile, in a minimum of six sessions. As we'll discuss later, these sessions should be completed three months before the wedding. They will continue periodic contact with the engaged couple leading up to the wedding and complete the vital post-wedding work during the year after the wedding. Usually the Mentor Couple will also participate, in some way, in the wedding ceremony (such as Bible reading).

The Wedding Coordinator

The Coordinator coordinates the wedding, period.[10]

Pastors should NEVER[11] preside over a wedding without a wedding Coordinator. Certainly, I've performed a few weddings on mountaintops and seashores where a Coordinator wasn't used. But I wish we'd had a Coordinator to keep all the pieces together.

When you recruit a Wedding Coordinator, don't just look for female candidates. Many men have great skills for the position. Look for a high quality (tasteful but not extravagant), passionate, organized, care-giving, gracious person to be your Coordinator.

Almost certainly, you will need to train any new Wedding Coordinator in a biblical understanding of weddings and the role of the pastor. They must be on the same theological and missional page as

---

9 www.FOCCUSINC.com offers on-line training for Mentor Couples.

10 If you have enough volunteers, consider a Reception Coordinator as well. A Wedding Coordinator might also be a Reception Coordinator, but NOT at the same wedding.

11 I know, never say never, but I cannot imagine performing a wedding without a good coordinator to guide the process. I've known pastors who tried to guide the wedding from the platform using head-nods and hand-signals. Dare I say, "That's just plain crazy!"?

the pastoral leadership. They must understand that the wedding is a worship service for the attending congregation, not a pageant set up to show off a bride's glimmering dress. A clear understanding, including how the Coordinator communicates with photographers, ushers, florists, etc., will set the stage for a great event and reduce the stress of the day.

In brief, the Wedding Coordinator is the church's representative (and partner with the presiding pastor) who works with the engaged couple, to make sure all details of the wedding day are completed on time and in an appropriate manner.

As we'll discuss later, the Wedding Coordinator will guide the wedding rehearsal, turning the rehearsal over to the pastor for the actual wedding service walk-through. The Coordinator is then responsible for guiding the recessional, and giving instructions for the wedding day. Before and all during the wedding, the Wedding Coordinator is just that, the coordinator—the *final word*.

If the Wedding Coordinator speaks, everyone **will** listen.

She or he gives direction to the entire process from beginning picture taking, to flower pinning, to processional, to the recessional, and getting the bridal party out of the wedding and to the reception. Since all the details on the wedding timeline have been previously agreed upon, the engaged couple only needs to follow directions at the rehearsal and wedding, not make decisions.[12]

The Marriage Ministry Coordinator

If you're a pastor, serving as the temporary Marriage Ministry Coordinator, plan to quickly replace yourself with a couple who is passionate about the success of marriages. They might be the first Mentor Couple as well.

The Marriage Ministry Coordinator will guide the overall Marriage Ministry emphasis of your congregation, which will probably include:

---

12 Rarely will decisions need to be reconsidered during the rehearsal. However, when "the plan" just doesn't work once everyone is together, the Wedding Coordinator will guide the engaged couple and pastor to make adjustments to the original plan. For example, if the standing positions for the attendants must be changed, due to unforeseen issues, the plan will be changed at the rehearsal.

- Training of the Mentor Couples, Wedding Coordinators, and Reception Coordinators, and continual mentoring for excellence in their ministries.
- Looking for relationship needs within the community of faith and attempting to network those needs with sources of help.
- Keeping the atmosphere of healthy relationships stirring on the front burner of the congregation's mind.

The Marriage Ministry Coordinator must live in a healthy marriage or have lived in one if they are now widowed. They should have the gifts of passionate-caregiving, along with basic organizational and communication skills.

A WORD ABOUT HONORARIUMS[13]

Paying congregational members for their ministry work is a mixed bag. Some positions need financial remuneration because the time needed to perform the task takes away from a person's regular source of income. I have only one strong bias about paying in a local congregation. I pay the lead person in the **nursery**, so the children see a common face each week (remember the nursery is the most important ministry in the church).

Around that lead person I recruit servants who rotate in and out over various weeks. We can never pay all persons for their ministries within and without a congregation and every Jesus-follower is called to serve in ministry. However, it is important that people know if they are to be paid and how much, right up front. It's better to have disappointed people at the beginning of the recruiting process than angry people whose expectations have not been met later on.

If you plan to hire one Marriage Ministry person to your staff, I'd suggest you put that money into the **Marriage Ministry Coordinator**. We've never had funds to pay a Marriage Ministry Coordinator. Instead I honor them at least once a year with a very nice dinner to say, "Thank You."

The **Mentor Couple** should be volunteers/servants from the congregation who receive an honorarium from the newly married couple.

---

13 For those who must have it, *honoraria* may be your preferred term but I discovered that dictionaries accept both versions of the plural for *honorarium*.

The **Wedding Coordinator** should also be a volunteer/servant from the congregations who receives an honorarium from the newly married couple.

The **Pastor** usually receives a salary from the congregational budget so performing a wedding is part of the pastoral duties. That said, couples will often present an honorarium to the pastor since the pastor is the one they've worked most closely with, and who is the most visible.

However, the pastor should become the voice for those behind-the-scenes persons who may be forgotten—

musicians,
maintenance engineers,
parking attendants,
technicians (and others)—

who often put in the most work but usually receive little or no recognition for their effort.[14]

Print a "Fees for Services" Guide

In order to keep expectations clear, work out a fee and honorarium plan with your governing board. Then print it. This guide should be in the Wedding Packet that you provide a couple at the first interview session.

---

14 You'll need to decide your own fee structure according to your community. But don't underestimate them. People pay thousands of dollars to photographers, florists, and cake bakers but often ignore people like musicians who have prepared for hours. If your ministry includes payment for the behind-the-scenes people in the wedding fees, there should be no further expectation of gifts.

A PLAN BIGGER THAN WEDDINGS

Now that we've explored some questions of Marriage Ministry and looked at potential team members to lead it, let's consider a basic ministry model that you can adapt to fit your context.

ONCE UPON AN ENGAGEMENT

Marriage researchers recommend six months to a full year of pre-marital preparation before a wedding. Engagements are often longer than that, since couples must reserve the reception hall at least a year ahead.[1]

When couples announce their engagements, they tend to throw financial caution to the wind, reserve their party location, then head to the church to get a date on the calendar. Frequently they arrive at a church office with little or no church background, assuming they can just announce the date they want to rent and it is done. That must not be true if we're committed to life-long marriages.

---

1 Wedding dates are often driven by party-house reservations. In the next chapter we will discuss antidotes for the **extravagant consumption** that so often identifies a wedding. As leaders, we can begin changing the expectations for weddings within and without our congregations.

INSTEAD, when a couple comes to the church to request a wedding date, they should be introduced to the church's wedding process—starting with a packet of materials that introduce them to your requirements for weddings, and your understanding of marriage. There should be *no pastoral appointment* until this packet has been *digested*. The packet can be as elaborate or simple as you desire. However, I've found that at least four pieces of material should be included. They seem to be read more thoroughly if in a brief, flyer format.

For the couples who come to you with no church or biblical background, this is a chance to graciously begin setting the stage for further discussions of faith issues and the purposes of marriage.

Consider this 10-step process:

STEP 1—WEDDING INFORMATION PACKET

[NOTE: Samples of several of the pieces that are mentioned in the following pages can be found in the Appendix, starting on page 125.]

The packet should include, at least, these five pieces:

A Wedding Overview Brochure that describes the wedding process in your congregation. Use a simple checklist that doesn't overwhelm the couple before you have time to talk with them in detail.

Your Policy on Divorce and Remarriage. Make sure your content is written in *encouraging, positive tones*. Couples working through divorce and remarriage don't need us adding guilt to an already difficult situation.

God's Plan for Sex, Including the Issue of Cohabitation. Again, we can choose to be a healing agent in the lives of two people who need your (and God's) help. We **must not** pry into a couple's sexual history. That history is a gift for only them to share and the glue that bonds them together. Our goal is to protect and strengthen that bond. Let the brochure describe God's creation dream for relationships and how couples can move back into a virginal state.

A Wedding Interview Information Form. This is my key document to use during the initial interview with an engaged couple. Most people (particularly the *macho* guys) can fake what you want to hear for an hour. When they must answer a pointed set of questions before the first meeting, it's harder to keep up the facade. You then have time to review their answers and prepare follow-up questions.

Stewarding God's Creation—a wedding in green. You have the opportunity to offer an alternative to the extravagance of most weddings. If you set a biblical stewardship model, you not only save the obscene consumption of non-renewable resources but may save a family from bankruptcy.

Gather a team of knowledgeable people to brainstorm a list of ideas that can be presented to the engaged couple's families. A list should include items, such as how to dress less expensively, avoiding family debt for the wedding and reception, and lower-cost reception locations.[2]

STEP 2—THE INITIAL PASTORAL INTERVIEW

When the *Wedding Interview Information Form* is returned and the pastor has prepared follow-up questions, the meeting is set with the engaged couple. This meeting is a time to get to know the couple better and decide if you *tentatively approve* performing the wedding. A final decision is made only after the premarital work is completed—approximately three months before the wedding.

Both the bride and groom should come to the interview **without** parents. Unless you make this clear to the couple (they are the two getting married and will both be integrally involved in the wedding preparation), you may end up with the bride and her mother, usually dragging along the latest bridal magazine.

During this initial interview, discussion will include topics like:

- Life-long marriage *takes priority* over a great wedding.
- Weddings are a Christian community worship event.
- The engaged couple's individual faith pilgrimages (Are they committed to Jesus as the center of their marriage?).
- The steps in the wedding preparation process. You will want to create a Wedding Checklist to cover the main items that a couple must complete up to the wedding, and the post-wedding requirements for meeting with the Mentor Couple.
- When and how you will work with the couple to create the wedding worship service.

---

2 Chapters 7 and 9 describe specific ideas that we have used as alternatives to extravagance while maintaining quality and appropriate elegance.

- A review of the *Wedding Packet* materials.
- A review of a *Wedding Handbook*—a resource you may want to provide for them to keep all the materials they'll be working with during the premarital days. Make sure it includes contact information for the Mentor Couple and the Wedding Coordinator.

Exclude Jesus?

If an engaged couple wants you to perform their wedding but they don't want anything *religious* or any of "that Jesus stuff," you have a difficult decision to make. Remember, that's about 60% of those who come to you for weddings.

Are you going to send them away or work with them as an agent of grace—doing the best you can to both serve them and be a witness of Jesus love?

Before you make the decision, there are several considerations that could change your whole ministry future:

- Why does the couple want you to perform the wedding rather than a judge?
- Is the couple open to all the premarital work that you require?
- Is the couple open to discussion of faith issues?
- Does the couple have at least a belief in a *higher power* or *creator of life*?
- Will you have opportunity to minister to the couple after the wedding?
- Is ministering to the many non-religious/non-Christian population part of your ministry call?

If a couple is open to the required premarital work, and has some openness to a Creator, I will try to work with them. I may be the only Jesus-follower whom they encounter; at least one who accepts them as they are. I don't apologize for who I am or what I believe. I gently state that right up front. But I never ask people to pretend they are Jesus-followers, just to get through a ceremony I create. Thus, I will not use "Jesus-talk" to describe a couple during the ceremony if they are not believers. If the couple is willing, I do share God's creation dream for relationships in general and couples specifically. It's amazing how much Good News you can include in a four-minute, carefully worded homily.

I trust the Holy Spirit to do God's work with the couple through our Marriage Ministry team, while we're in the marriage preparation process. And sometimes people become Jesus-followers because they've experienced Jesus during the months leading up to the wedding.

If you don't find a way to work with the non-believing 60%, you'll miss a whole boat-load of scary situations AND exciting Kingdom opportunities.

STEP 3—FOLLOWING THE INITIAL INTERVIEW

Upon leaving the interview, with pastoral approval, the engaged couple must immediately get to work lining up appointments with a Mentor Couple and a Wedding Coordinator.

The **Wedding Coordinator** will begin compiling the basic wedding information and keep the couple on task toward completion by the wedding date. The Coordinator will work back and forth between the engaged couple and the church to make sure all the details are carried out appropriately.

The **Mentor Couple** meets with the engaged couple for a get-acquainted session and introduces them to the marriage profile that your congregation has chosen. The engaged couple will then complete the profile forms on the internet with results returned to the Mentor Couple. Once the results are back, the Mentor Couple and engaged couple will meet for at least six more sessions to work through the profile. All sessions are to be completed before the *Three Month Check-in*.[3]

STEP 4—AN ENGAGED ENCOUNTER WEEKEND

Engaged Encounter is a specific program for helping engaged couples look at their relationship in its current state and where it needs to grow for life-long success. You may have another option that accomplishes the same goal. Whatever your options, all engaged couples need to experience a guided weekend away together, to seriously examine their future. If you are unable to provide the weekend yourself (I've only served in one church that did), then partner with someone who does provide such a weekend. An internet search will direct you to where an *Engaged Encounter* or similar weekend is held.

3 This is discussed in STEP 5.

STEP 5—THE THREE-MONTH CHECK-IN

At the three-months-to-go-before-the-wedding date, the team (Wedding Coordinator, the Mentor Couple and the pastor) must have a face-to-face meeting, to discuss whether the wedding is a *go*, a *no-go*, a *postpone* or some variation. This three-month window provides a space—before invitations are sent, clothing ordered, and gifts purchased—if issues surface with the engaged couple. It's probably the last point to cancel or delay a wedding with minimal embarrassment for the engaged couple and their families.

STEP 6A—THE WEDDING IS A "GO"

If the team decides that this wedding should go forward, then the date is *inked in* on the church calendar. If it appears that there is need for further counseling or more complete counseling than the Mentor Couple can provide, it should be started immediately. The pastor will discuss the options with the engaged couple as to whether they want to proceed as planned, put a hold on the wedding date, or wait until they've had discussions with the counselor.

STEP 6B—THE WEDDING IS A "NO GO" OR "POSTPONE"

If the result of the *Three-Month Check-in* is cancellation or postponement of the wedding, painful decisions lie ahead for all involved. The pastor will need to tell the engaged couple what decision the team believes is best. The engaged couple may be relieved to know that the team has discovered issues they were already experiencing. On the other hand, the engaged couple may choose to go somewhere else to be married by another pastor or government official.

The pastor has a dilemma—whether or not to perform the wedding against the team's advice, believing that if the wedding is performed in the church, future ministry and healing may be possible. This will prove to be a most difficult ministry scenario, needing an abundance of prayer.

STEP 7—CHARGING TO THE WEDDING

Once the date is confirmed on the church calendar, the pastor must step back into the picture with the engaged couple. It's time to create a great wedding worship, together. The pastor will supply the couple with several sample worship orders they can cut and paste together to best represent what they want the wedding to look like. Later, the pastor will meet again with the engaged couple to begin refining the worship order. Remember, as the spiritual leader of the congregation, the pastor reserves the right to direct the content of the wedding in biblical ways. However, don't be afraid of creativity. In the next chapter, we'll discuss some wonderful variations on the wedding theme.

The pastor will use the opportunities of wedding discussion to delve more deeply into the engaged couple's spiritual growth and life. The couple may also be willing to discuss sexual issues more openly with the pastor than with the Mentor Couple. However, do not attempt to *violate* a person or couple by prying too deeply into their sexual past or difficult issues.

We must attempt to give guidance or answer questions. Beyond that, if significant issues arise, referral to a counselor is the best choice. Let me add, engaged couples **do** rate the private time with the pastor very highly.[4] Thus it must be treasured and used well.

In the meantime, the Mentor Couple will continue to interact socially with the engaged couple. After working through the premarital profile, most Mentor Couples are so well invested with the engaged couple for social interactions to come naturally. This continuing contact will set the stage for a successful year of post-wedding follow-up.

STEP 8—THE WEDDING REHEARSAL

Working through a rehearsal is something of an awkward dance unless the pastor and the Wedding Coordinator are closely working from the same *script*. In the next chapter we will discuss specific details for a successful rehearsal. For now, let's just say that the Wedding Coordinator gets all wedding participants into and out of their wedding posi-

---

4 "An Empirical Approach to Designing Marriage Preparation Programs" by Lee Williams, Lisa A. Riley, Gail S. Risch, and David T. Van Dyke, *The American Journal of Family Therapy* (Brunner/Mazel, 1999) 27: 276.

tions. The pastor guides the actual worship order. A couple of walk-throughs should be sufficient.

STEP 9—THE WEDDING DAY

Trust your Wedding Coordinator. The Coordinator should have a printout of all scheduled times and events for the day. Remember that she or he should be guiding the entire process from pinning flowers to sending people down the aisle. The pastor's role is to calmly guide the worship order: keeping alert to potential fainters, reminding the couple of specific directions (e.g. how to hold their hands for the rings), and leading the congregation in great celebration worship.

Something always goes wrong at weddings. The pastor's role is to anticipate what might go wrong and work quickly for a solution. Most people will not remember the mistake if it is handled effectively.

STEP 10—THE FIRST CRITICAL YEAR

After the wedding-dust settles, the Mentor Couple will re-engage with the newly married couple, at least on an infrequent basis. The first year of marriage is the most critical for life-long marriage survival. And this may be the most important role the Mentor Couple plays.

> [We've found] the primary emphasis of our work has been premarital, neomarital, and early marriage education. Why? Primarily because research has shown that half of all serious marital problems develop in the first two years of marriage.... A unique feature of the [SYMBIS (Saving Your Marriage Before It Starts)] program includes the Marriage Mentor Club which links newlyweds with a seasoned married couple throughout the first year of their marriage.[5]

5 From "The SYMBIS Approach to Marriage Education" by Les Parrott III and Leslie Parrott, *Journal of Psychology and Theology,* 32:3 (Biola University, Rosemead School of Psychology, 2001), 208.

If your congregation is unable to attach a Mentor Couple to every newly married couple for the first year, Dr. David Olson suggests starting a Caring Community of Couples.[6] This CCC is a small group of newly marrieds (just married to two years) who meet together regularly with a Mentor Couple, to discuss marriage and life issues. If your congregation is small enough or has too few newly married couples, join with couples from other partner churches.

We found that before nine months into the marriage we didn't have much impact in a couple's relationship. Certainly, there are difficult times as the couple works through the blending of their life patterns. Yet, nearer 12 months of marriage it's time to guide the newly married couple through a post-marriage profile, e.g. REFOCCUS or ENRICH (both mentioned previously). After the Mentor Couple has presented the profile and the newly married couple has completed it, the Mentor Couple will compare the premarital profile and the post-marital profiles to see where growth has taken place and where growth is still needed.

The Mentor Couple will not usually complete as many post-marital sessions as during the premarital work. It will depend on the needs that present themselves. Usually one or two sessions will help to work through any issues. If deeper issues have come forward during the first year, it is wise to press a new couple toward professional marriage counseling. There is no better time than the present to head off deeper crises that may develop in flawed marriage patterns.

6 See more at www.prepare-enrich.com, P.O. Box 190, Minneapolis, MN 55440; 800.331.1661.

7

CREATING GREAT WEDDINGS

"Most of [an engaged couple's] energy is focused on the wedding, and they are really not thinking about what kind of marriage they're going to have…. Couples invest too much in their wedding, which lasts only one day, rather than in their marriage which is intended to last a lifetime."[1]

To repeat, as ministry leader, you're the primary person responsible for implementing the creation of a wedding, so you should be meeting with the bride and groom, not either set of parents. At the beginning, some grooms will find it uncomfortable to participate in the wedding planning, but they are integral to the process.

At the initial interview with the couple, I explain that I'm not overly concerned about the wedding. The ceremony won't be perfect—they never are—but we'll get them married. It will be a great event; a *community* event including God, family, and friends. Certainly we'll be marrying a couple, but the focus is not the wedding; the primary focus is on launching a healthy, life-long marriage.

---

1   From an interview by David Olson in *USA Today* (May 3, 2005) in regards to the much-publicized story of a bride who ran away from the stresses of her wedding and marriage.

We've already discussed some of the issues you'll need to consider if you're performing the wedding for a non-Christian couple. The following comments are primarily directed toward a wedding where the engaged couple has some church or faith background. If the couple you're working with has no faith or church background, please interpret all comments for your specific context. Some will work and some will not.

Whatever else your role in the couple's life, it is first spiritual.

If the bride and groom are not sure of their faith in Jesus, this is the time to help them understand what personal faith is.

Help them understand what a wedding worship is.

Help them understand what a Christian home looks like.

All this must be integrated into the pre-marital work that the pastor and Mentor Couple do during the six months before the wedding.

When using a Wedding Information Packet, there is no mistake about where we're headed when the couple arrives for the first interview. Their party-house date and bridal-magazine expectations will not be driving the discussion.[2] We can then talk about what a Jesus-follower's wedding and reception look like. Of course, most family members and friend will want a voice the wedding plans. But from the outset, the couple needs to know the foundation we're working from. You may even need to set a special session with parents to explain their roles.

USE THE ENGAGEMENT WISELY

Engagement is usually the most stressful time in any relationship—more than marriage.

Couples are dreaming of the day they'll be officially married. If they're not already sexually active, the pressure is building for sexual involvement—they've gone on record as committed to one another for life. In their minds they're "already married."

They are planning a wedding and too many people are giving direction for how it should happen.

---

2   This is an opportunity to teach several stewardship principles to the couple. You can alert them to the options of renting lower-cost reception facilities such as your church hall. You may help them break free from the "expectation cycle" they may feel pressured to follow.

Often, one or both the bride and groom are in school.

Differing preferences and expectations come to the surface.

All this adds extreme tension and over-blown conflicts may arise between the two. You can help diffuse this stress by acknowledging it up front, and offering your listening ear when everyone else is talking.

In the middle of this engagement pressure cooker, I encourage couples *not* to spend lengthy times alone in deep spiritual sharing. Since our sexuality and spirituality are so intertwined, a couple can easily become sexually involved during intimate spiritual sharing. Thus, they should avoid devotional times in secluded places.

In my discussions with several counselors, there has not been consensus on this topic, but let me raise one more caution.

Engaged couples should avoid intense times discussing their sexual history with one another very long before marriage, except under the guidance of a counselor. As discussed previously, pastors should not pry into an individual's sexual past.

On the other hand, this age of multiple STDs compels couples to share their past with their partner, and to complete a thorough physical exam, so neither partner is hiding a past involvement until after the wedding.[3]

STOP MORTGAGING THE FUTURE

What most families spend on a wedding (and reception) is scandalous. Too often the wedding is designed for great photography or to meet expectations from our various publics. [4]

Alan Hirsch describes the dilemma and opportunity we face as Jesus-followers in the 21st century. This is just as true for those who

---

3   Another topic you will need to explore with the couple is past or current use of **pornography** by either partner. Pornography creates major relational challenges both before and after the wedding. So, gently ask the tough questions.

4   In the summer of 2009, my youngest daughter finished her wedding plans on a limited budget. The year before, our oldest daughter married. Five years before that, our son married his college sweetheart while they were both in school with little income. So I know I'm right. Depending on the number of volunteers, and what can be borrowed, a wonderful wedding and reception can be created for between $5,000 and $12,000 (you might adjust slightly for inflation). The latest data reports the average USAmerican wedding to cost $28,400. That's an overcharge of at least $16,000 that should be put into a house payment, purchase of a car, savings, or someone's credit card debt.

have no commitment to Jesus. He says,

> *"I have come to believe that the major threat to the viability of our*
> *faith is that of consumerism.... Much of that which goes by the name*
> *of advertising is an explicit offer to a sense of identity, meaning,*
> *purpose, and community"—replacing the true foundation of identity,*
> *meaning, purpose and community with a counterfeit. Rather than*
> *advertising that describes the true attributes of a product, "advertising*
> *has everything to do with managing the value and significance people*
> *give to products and the relative status we derive from them.... Under*
> *this excessive influence of the market, experiences, indeed life itself,*
> *tends to become commodified; ...people are viewed as mere consump-*
> *tive units. The suburbs all orbit around the central consumerist temple*
> *called The Shopping Mall. Teenagers walk aimlessly up and down*
> *these soulless corridors as if looking for an answer that somehow evades*
> *them in the windows. Their parents saunter through the same malls*
> *indulging in a dose of 'retail therapy.' "[5]*

So, it's no wonder when couples and parents arrive at our door-
steps, traumatized by the anticipated need to match the Smiths'
wedding—dismayed at how to borrow for it. We have the potential
to make a huge difference in a couple's future if we can guide a family
into a biblical stewardship model of weddings.

Often non-believers are more concerned about creation care and
excessive spending than professed believers. So, don't fear the discussion with all couples, although you may need to intervene between the
engaged couple and their parents, who wish to impress their friends.

If couples will set a budget for the wedding and reception, and
live within it, they can create a wedding and reception within reasonable costs. All vendors (e.g. photographers, florists, rental companies,
etc.) will push a couple to the point of extravagance. They are slick
in their gimmicks, using words like, "It's traditional to..." or "You will
want to...." The most difficult issue in planning the events surrounding a wedding is meeting the expectations of advertisers, outsiders, and

---

5 For a dynamic approach to living faith in the 21ˢᵗ century, read *The Forgotten Ways: Reactivat-*
   ing the Missional Church by Alan Hirsch (Grand Rapids: Brazos Press, 2006). These comments
   were collected from pages 106–109.

family members. As pastor, you may be a solo voice in helping couples stand up to the pressure and say, "NO."

CREATE A BIBLICAL WORSHIP CELEBRATION

If the couple you're working with is Jesus-followers, you will guide them in creating a Christian-community worship celebration. As discussed earlier, if the couple has no Christian-faith commitment, you will need to work more gently in the wedding creation.

Either way, the pastor has the final word on what is included in a wedding. You are commissioned or ordained as the ministry leader to ensure that all the needed segments of the service are in place and done appropriately. That doesn't call for setting up a dictatorship, however. Giving a couple creative latitude in designing the various worship sections is vital if they are to own it, but you must make sure that what is included fits your theology and biblical interpretation.[6]

Make sure the wedding worship matches what you believe about creation, Jesus and healthy relationships.

Given to Each Other

For example, after reading the earlier chapters you know where I stand on the lies we've taught about women being lorded over by men.

Sadly, many weddings still have the bride given away to the groom; her hand taken from the father's authority and handed to the groom's authority. Sometimes ignorantly, this symbol is continuing a practice that demonstrates fallen humanity—the sin of the first man and first woman. Why not encourage brides and grooms to be given to each other by their families? Neither is property of the other. Both are a gift of God to the other, with God as the authority, so let the wedding worship say so.

What a magnificent statement when families walk the aisle with their child to bless them and present them to their soon-to-be spouse!

6 To repeat myself. after approving the wedding at the Three-Month Check-in, I give several sample weddings to the engaged couple with an outline of what parts are usually included in a wedding worship—and what parts are mandatory. (See a sample on page 142.) We set an appointment, about two weeks out, for them to report back what parts they want to "cut and paste" to create their own wedding order. Then we negotiate the various parts until the final version is completed.

Without announcing theological or biblical views, let the wedding symbolism demonstrate God's plan for humanity. You will not convince couples to do everything the way you want it in a wedding. So, choose carefully which issues are truly theological and which are just traditional or personal preferences.

Write a Full Script

If you're like me, you get emotionally involved when leading worship, particularly weddings and funerals. So I will do neither without a full script. (There's a sample wedding script in the Appendix.) Most weddings provide a worship folder or program for the attendees. That's not enough content for you as the worship leader if your eyes tear up or if something doesn't go as planned—as usually (dare I say "always") happens in a wedding.

When writing my script I include every word anyone might say.

For example, all scriptures that will be read are fully printed in my script. I learned from experience when a scripture reader didn't appear for the wedding, and we couldn't find a Bible on the stage because the custodian had put them into storage for the wedding, that someone needs to have a copy of the Scriptures.[7]

Because tears flow easily from me, and I'm an introvert, I don't want to worry about what I'll say after I regain my composure. I want to take a couple of breaths, regain my composure, and go back to the words I'm reading. This is not to say that I always follow the script. Particularly in a homily, I can usually speak without the notes, but I have them just in case.

When introducing a couple to the congregation for the first time, I always use my notes, especially if it's my daughter who I'm introducing as the wife of a man whose last name I don't usually attach to her first name.

If you preach from a manuscript, using a script for a wedding will be very natural. If you use an outline for preaching, which I usually do, you may need to practice looking up and staying connected to the congregation. The key to using a script is to *not* sound like you're reading a script.

---

7   How embarrassing to find no Bibles in a church. Fortunately the bride's father had one he could hand me. I found the correct reference, read the scripture and we went on to conclude a great wedding.

Don't Get Run Down by a Drive-Through Wedding

Like me, you've attended weddings so short that you barely sat down before the recessional started and the couple dashed out the door to the reception. It was almost like the wedding was the warm-up for the party. Don't let that happen, even if the couple can hardly wait to get to the dance and on to bed. Plan for the wedding to last a minimum of *one hour*. There is no hurry in worship.

Again, if you're working with a couple who are not Jesus-followers, the wedding will naturally be shorter since you won't include some of the additional worship material. But don't rush to get done. We're setting the stage for a life-long marriage, not a pre-show for a party.

Then There's the Music

A huge variety of love and wedding music is available. If you search the internet, hundreds of song titles will appear. Almost none express Jesus' view of love or marriage. The pastor will need great wisdom in guiding a couple through the selection of music. Remember, tradition is not always the best.[8] For example, the Bridal March ("Here comes the bride...") harkens back to the pagan view of the bride coming as a chosen trophy, arriving for the groom's pleasure.

A good test for whether a song is Christian isn't the beat, it's source or the composer. It's about the words. Do they express a healthy love between a man and woman? Are they *other* centered? The song title may not be known as Christian but the words may express God's love, so why not use it? And don't fear the romantic.

Congregational Participation

Including the congregation in the wedding worship celebration is critical. At a minimum, the community of faith should sing together. In addition they could read scripture—in unison or responsively—participate in a candle lighting ceremony, or affirm vows to support the newly-married couple. The goal is to move people from simply observers to worship participants.

---

8   I'm a 1960s kid, so tradition is not part of my vocabulary. However, as a musician I have deep appreciation for all styles of music, from all eras of history. None is more sacred than another. Much of what is called *contemporary Christian* music is not very Christian—but rather is very egocentric ("What has Jesus done for me lately?").

Include Holy Communion (Eucharist)

Pastors from liturgical churches may skip this section; you'll automatically preside over Holy Communion as a part of your Wedding Mass.

Those of us in less formal congregations often get a request from the engaged couple to take Holy Communion by themselves as the first act of their marriage. It doesn't cross their minds that Holy Communion is for the entire Christian church—the faith community.

After I explain that the Eucharist is for all Christians, NEVER just the wedding party or bride and groom, I always get the next question, "How long will it take if everyone participates?"

The simple answer is, "Not long, depending on how we serve."

The follow-up question from Christian couples is, "What do we do about people who are not Christians, so they're not embarrassed?"

My response, "The same thing we do every time Holy Communion is served during any worship service. We offer it to all but don't point out those who are not taking."

Intinction—The solution to the questions of timeliness and non-believers in the audience is to serve by intinction. If you're not familiar with the term, it's where congregational attendees receive a piece of the bread and then dip it in the wine cup. The congregation should be alerted as to whether you will be using grape juice, wine or both. Labeling the wine is always a good idea.

Saving time—The key in serving the Eucharist is setting up enough serving stations for the elements. You will need one person for the bread and one for the cup at each station. The pastor(s) must also remain alert to become additional servers if a lengthy line builds at any one station.

The pastor should serve the servers first, then the bride, groom and attendants. The attendants should be seated, particularly if there are those who will not partake. The bride and groom will probably move to a kneeler.

Protecting The Identity of Non-Participants—Allow a congregational "free-for-all." Direct people to partake at their nearest station when they are ready. **NEVER** usher rows of people to the communion stations. With the attendants seated, non-participants will not be noticed, reducing any embarrassment.[9] For those who may find physical difficulty in moving to a serving station, verbally offer to serve anyone in their seats if they will let a server know of their desire to partake.

The pastor should brief both the attendants as to how the Eucharist will be performed and affirm any who are uncomfortable partaking, so they know to let the elements go by. Attendants may also alert the pastor before the wedding of their desire to not be served.

Choosing servers—According to your tradition, this may be a no-brainer. However, if there is flexibility in who may serve the Communion elements, this is a good place to include people who have a special relationship to the bride and groom. You might consider the Mentor Couple, attendants, family members, a youth group, or close friends.

Explore Creative Options

Set the wedding in the round—Arranging the venue in the round symbolizes the best biblical view as it incorporates the entire congregation into the worship experience. In the round, the couple faces outward toward the witnesses (usually elevated, most of the time), so they can see the bride's and groom's faces, and hear them, when they promise to live together, forever. As pastor, you will be the *facilitator of worship,* usually working from the congregational level. The down-side of facing the congregation is that the bride's train will not be visible for photography. You'll have to pose that picture later.

Move People Around—Feel free to move people around or have the attendants sit down during part of the service, such as during the Eucharist. No rules (except maybe tradition) say that bridesmaids and groomsmen must tempt passing out for the wedding to be a success. It's only good for the humorous family videos at some later date.

---

9   There are several reasons persons may choose to abstain from Holy Communion. They may not be Jesus followers. They may feel uncomfortable participating outside of their own faith tradition. They may have physical difficulty holding the Communion elements or moving to a station. The may just not want to participate. So, no pressure.

> *Since brides, grooms and pastors usually move during the*
> *wedding, keeping the blood flowing in their legs, they have*
> *less chance of passing out. On the other hand, attendants*
> *often feel the need to remain statuesque. Remind them to*
> *frequently flex their knees if they cannot move or be seated.*

Unity Candles[10]—Unity candles have become traditional in most weddings, being lit from the family candles.

And family candles are NOT blown out. The couple is not breaking relation with their family of origin. Instead they are extending their heritage to the next generation.

In one wedding, candles were lit for the grandparents who were not present. Another set were lit by the grandparents in attendance. Then a final set—the family candles—were lit by parents. The family candles were used to light the unity candle.

> *Always give directions to the congregation, as you would*
> *do at any other candle-lighting event. Remind the partici-*
> *pants to keep the lighted flame upright, leaning the unlit*
> *candle into the flame of the lit candle. Did I mention to*
> ***watch those bridal veils around candle flames?***

Mixing Sand—If you've not seen colored sand mixed to represent the unifying of two persons, it works well as an outdoor version of the

---

10 Lighted candles and bridal veils together terrify me. Brides with face-covering veils should never blow out candles. Remind all wedding attendants that veils are explosive. Always check for the nearest fire extinguisher and anticipate ripping a burning veil off a bride.

unity candle or as a variation indoors. The pastor should have a vial of sand (representing God at the center of the relationship) to mix with the couple's vials. Thus, three colors of sand will mix together in the carafe. Setting the carafe on a slowly rotating base helps to intermix the colors and create a more artistic effect.

The sand also serves as a symbol of creation-unity, harkening back to the first man and woman (*adam*) brought up from the sand of the earth.

Commissioning for Ministry—Every Jesus follower is called to ministry. If a couple wants to symbolize their call to ministry, congregational candle lighting can be a significant part of a wedding celebration.

For the commissioning, the unity candle can stand as the Christ-candle (Jesus the center of the marriage relationship) from which the couple will light a new set of candles. Those candles represent the light of Jesus living through them, going out into the world. The bride and groom (attendants or whomever they choose) then move throughout the congregation, lighting candles for each attendee. This candle-lighting time will also include a commissioning prayer for the couple.

Include the Reception[11] —Worship does not end once we leave a worship center. Worship is our continuous response of Jesus-followers to God. It is our whole lives, including the wedding reception. So before leaving the worship room, invite the attendees to continue worship when moving to the reception.

Don't let the wedding and reception become disconnected. They are parts of a whole. The music, the food, the conversation, the dancing are all part of celebrating God's bringing this man and this woman together. So we celebrate with thanksgiving for what God has done; anticipating what God will continue to do in their (and our) lives.

---

11 These comments will be true, if the reception is **open for all attendees**. If the reception is only for **invited guests**, you may want to announce the continuation of worship once guests have arrived at the reception site.

8

REHEARSING WITHOUT FAMILY FIGHTS

If you're a wedding pro, you probably have your own plan for wedding rehearsals. If you're new to weddings, this model will give you a place to start until you create your own plan.

PASTORS DON'T SKIP REHEARSALS

I know pastors who assume that their role for a wedding is meeting with the couple once or twice prior to the wedding, then arriving on wedding day in time to read their pastoral part and leave. I also know not all weddings bring excitement to the pastor, when you've performed dozens of them.

However, as you've noted from this entire book, the pastor is an integral part of the wedding worship. The pastor works in tandem with the Wedding Coordinator to lead the rehearsal. As pastors, we are committed to a life of ministry with the couple we are marrying, so we will never miss the rehearsal.

COORDINATING THE REHEARSAL

The Wedding Coordinator will work out any specific issues (and all facets of the wedding order on the timeline) with the bride, groom, and pastor, before the rehearsal. Only decisions about unforeseen issues should be made at the rehearsal.

One of the greatest tension producers in a rehearsal is to ask the bride and groom to make decisions on the spot. They are under too much anxiety to do it gracefully. The Wedding Coordinator and pastor must exude confidence that all will be well during the wedding, assuring the bride and groom that if something goes astray the two of you will make it work out right. They can relax and follow your directions.

THE REHEARSAL ORDER

The wedding attendants (anyone who has a role in the wedding) are almost never all on time to a rehearsal. People straggle in for up to 30 minutes after the planned start time. Therefore, plan the rehearsal to last 1.5 hours, leaving plenty of drive time to the rehearsal dinner that usually follows. The pastor and Wedding Coordinator can use the wait-time to review final details with various participants, refine sound and light setups, explain the guidelines to the photographer or videographer, etc. It's also a good time to get acquainted with the wedding attendants as they arrive.

Once Everyone Is Gathered

The pastor will call the rehearsal to order and open with a prayer of blessing and a reminder to the attendants that the wedding is a worship service. She or he should review the expectations for those who help lead: whether singing, reading, or witnessing the wedding as a bridesmaid or groomsman. General announcements can be made here as well.

Family and Friends—The pastor will ask the bride and groom to introduce all attendants and family members to one another. Provide stick-on name tags and markers for each person as they arrive. This makes for an easy way to give directions to strangers—and for family members and attendants to get acquainted.

The Wedding Coordinator—The pastor will introduce the Wedding Coordinator as the overseer for the wedding, so "we will all pay attention to what she or he tells us to do." From that point on the Wedding Coordinator guides the rehearsal and all the details.

The Initial Walk-through—The Wedding Coordinator will call the attendants to an initial walk-through, describing how to get to their various standing positions. Once everyone has found their proper place for each section of the ceremony, the attendants will exit the worship center for a total run-through.

The Worship Order—When everyone has returned to their places, the pastor takes leadership of the rehearsal. The pastor will guide through each part of the wedding worship (reading only the beginning and ending of each section, including the vows) pausing for the coordinator to adjust attendants' positions as necessary. In other words, tell the couple and attendants what you are going to do, don't take time to do it all.

A Second Walk-through—If the worship order is complicated, it may be necessary to ease everyone's mind with a quick, second walk-through. Then offer time for questions and answers. Again, assure the groom, bride, and attendants that you will guide them through the wedding, so they can relax and follow your lead. Remind them that you carry a full script and know what is to happen in each portion of the worship.

The Marriage License—If you do not have a pattern for getting the marriage license signed and delivered, make sure to get it from the bride and groom at the rehearsal. Depending on your state laws, alert the signers you will need, to gather immediately following the wedding to sign the document.

You are responsible for filing the completed license with the proper authorities, once the wedding is over. Also, make several extra copies. One for your files; another copy should go into the married couple's hands as soon as possible—probably at the reception—for them to take on the honeymoon.

TRAIN THE USHERS

The Wedding Coordinator (if necessary the pastor) should guide each usher through a practice on how to graciously greet guests (the usher greets first, not waiting to be spoken to), how to help persons (usually the woman in a couple) hold his or her arm, how to stop at the seating place, and guide the people to a seat. A sample Usher Guide is available in the Resource Section. A printed card, handed to each usher, will increase the chances of their remembering what you tell them. (See sample instructions in the Appendix.)

COACH THE FLORISTS

Reputable florists will know the ropes for working with a bride, groom, and Wedding Coordinator. They couldn't stay in business if they didn't. The Wedding Coordinator should confirm that the bride or groom have set the proper time for flowers to arrive and for the florist to be out of the worship center. Sometimes florists need a reminder from the Wedding Coordinator. The pastor should only be a backup if the coordinator needs help. On the wedding day, the Wedding Coordinator will meet the florist and take responsibility for distribution of flowers to the proper people.

INSTRUCT THE PHOTOGRAPHER

I once stepped into our worship center for a rehearsal, to meet the grandfather of the bride, with whom I was to share the wedding leadership. I saw an older man on the stage, walked up and greeted him. He met me warmly as I told him how thankful I was to do this wedding with him. Immediately he began to tell me of changes we would need to make in the worship order and the various places he wanted the bride and groom to stand. Being a patient person I explained to the "grandfather" that we had spent extensive time planning the worship order and it was too late to make major changes.

He responded that he just couldn't get the pictures he wanted if we didn't make the changes.

Yep, he was the photographer, not the grandfather!

So, in my kindest, pastoral way, I told him that this was a worship service not a photo shoot, and that he was to leave the stage immediately and I didn't expect to see him near the stage again.

You may have guessed! I have an issue with photographers and videographers.

Usually—and I mean most of the time—they act as if they believe the wedding is about them. They will crawl on the floor behind the pastors or attendants. They will shoot flash pictures all through the event. They will walk up and down the aisles as they desire. But not at my weddings, nor should they at yours.

Good photographers can capture great moments and stay out of sight, without flash, once the bride and groom are in place. If a photographer needs to be up front during the actual ceremony, they either don't understand that a wedding is a worship event, are not professional, or their equipment is sub-par.

I sit down with the photographer just before the wedding and lay out the parameters of what they are allowed to do.[1] (See sample photographer/videographer instructions in the Appendix.)

They may stand in the aisle as the attendants and bride and groom enter; even use flash. They may take their usual candid pictures of the bridal party in preparation—in the dressing rooms, talking with family, etc.

Once the pastor(s) begins leading the worship, the flash is turned off and the photographer disappears, not to be seen again until the bride and groom recess out after the benediction.

Never is a photographer allowed in front of the worshipping congregation to shoot pictures. Long-range lenses work well.

Missed poses can be reset during the photo session following the wedding worship.

Leave enough time, before and after the wedding, for the photographer to do her work. The Wedding Coordinator and photographer must make sure that the timeline provides appropriate time for the photographer to meet the newly marrieds' wishes. Professional photographers will prepare a list of the couple's desired photos to shoot, but the Wedding Coordinator may need to assist the photographer in getting people into place, or if the bride, groom start requesting many additional shots.[2]

---

1 This conversation will be done by the Wedding Coordinator if the photographer attends the rehearsal. The Coordinator is usually too busy to have the conversation on the wedding day. Also, some photographers will not take the Coordinator seriously, so I have to "pull rank." Photographers have one chance to get it right or you should not allow them to be used again in your ministry center.

2 Emily T. Smith, professional wedding photographer.

We recently attended a small wedding using two photographers. They started at the front to photograph the bridal party processional. When the attendants, and bride and groom were in place, they stood among the bridesmaids and groomsmen, one on each side, shooting flash pictures of the pastor and bridal couple. After a few moments they moved to the front seats where they stood flashing pictures for the remainder of the wedding.

None of us who attended that wedding can remember much about it, but we hadn't planned on a photo demonstration.

If a photographer decides to ignore the guidelines, a pastor must stop the wedding and kindly ask the photographer to either leave or go to the back, out of sight.

Of Course They Want Videos

Videographers want to shoot great pictures of the wedding and there are a couple of options that work well.

One, set up cameras in the best photo spot on tripods behind plants or other visual barriers. A few minutes before the wedding begins, a designated person can turn the cameras on and let them run throughout the wedding.

Another possibility is to allow a person to stand/sit by a tripod, out of sight, and run a video camera during the service. Under no circumstances should the camera operator be moving around or trying to get better shots once the worship has begun.

A Final Thought About Photography

Most pictures of the wedding party should be taken before the ceremony.

Some brides and grooms want to preserve the tradition of not seeing each other before arriving at the altar, so pictures of the men and women can be taken separately. Gathering families, for the big family shot, must usually happen after the wedding worship since not everyone can arrive early enough to get into the picture.

After the wedding, plan the photography time for no more than one hour, if there is a public reception to immediately follow.

Brides and grooms forget that people have been hanging around for at least a half hour before the wedding, through the ceremony (about one hour), during the dismissal time (probably 30 minutes), then during the after-wedding photography session (another one-hour segment).

That adds up to around three hours; not long for a bride and groom but an eternity for guests who may start leaving the reception as soon as the bride and groom arrive.

A WELL-PLANNED REHEARSAL

There are many details to cover during a rehearsal, but working from a checklist and wisely using every minute, a rehearsal can be completed in less than two hours. And everyone will be pleased, even if they are still a little anxious about the wedding day itself. Let nerves be from anticipation of a life-changing day, not from uncertainty about details of the wedding worship.

9

PARTY TIME—
A THRIVING RECEPTION

If you have a respected voice with the couple whom you're marrying, you may be able to speak a word of sanity into their reception. However, you will have to speak early (and offer continued guidance, if they accept it) because volumes of people want a piece of the action. Much like a lottery winner, the pressure from family, friends, and vendors quickly overwhelms couples.

THINK ELEGANTLY SIMPLE

The reception is usually the financial sink-hole of an entire wedding experience. It was probably the 1990s when receptions changed from the punch and cake model (usually some mints, nuts and a few other finger foods) to a full-course dinner model. And out of necessity to pay for these over-the-top events, families have often mortgaged their futures, and the new couple's future.

I doubt that one crazy pastor (me) writing a book like this will turn the tide against extravagance. But don't get me wrong... with two daughters and a son, we've lived through the struggles of applying good stewardship principles to weddings and receptions.

It's not easy but it is possible to bring spending within reason.

But since you're not paying for the reception (unless it's one of your family members getting married) why should you care?

The fact is, as a congregational leader, you can help lower the bar on reception spending just as you will be leading the wedding planning. Because you care about your congregational families you can offer them freedom from the tyranny of overspending as they bring all areas of their lives into Jesus' perspective.

What might happen if your leadership team began to educate your congregation, maybe even with a sermon or two, about how to live as Christian stewards? What if you used weddings as an example of extreme waste; a place where families can rise against the consumerism tide?

RECRUIT A RECEPTION COORDINATOR

I didn't say hire a coordinator. In some circumstances hiring may be necessary, but usually there is someone in the bride and groom's circle of acquaintances—if your ministry center doesn't have such a person available—who can manage a social event. One key, of course, is finding a gracious person who understands living within a budget, resists the pressure for extravagance, and can carry an idea to completion.

A good Reception Coordinator will:

Be objective and say "No" when pressed by a vendor or the couple to spend more than the budget allows.

Recruit a team of people who will take the dream of a bride and groom, turn it into reality (and tear it down) without the bride and groom (or their families) becoming deeply involved.

This means that the bride and groom must let go of managing all the details themselves. Obviously, the coordinator will regularly check details with the engaged couple to make sure that he or she is on track with developing the dream.

Guide the reception (usually with an emcee, a DJ and/or pastor) to keep the reception activities on schedule.[1]

Newly marrieds will usually want to extend the reception beyond reasonable time. As described earlier, they tend to assume that attend-

---

1   The Reception Coordinator will produce a detailed timeline for the various activities at the reception just as the Wedding Coordinator did. For those not familiar with the terms: MC=master of ceremonies (announces what's happening next and makes introductions), DJ=disk jockey (plays the music and often acts as the MC).

ees desire to party for hours, like they do. The Coordinator will set a specific time or prescribed point (e.g. when one-third of the guests have departed) to announce the bride and groom's departure, and get them out the door while there are still enough guests to blow bubbles (or throw seeds) as they begin their honeymoon.

DROP THE MEAL DEAL

Despite what bridal magazines prescribe, couples are not obligated to provide a multi-course sit-down meal, no matter the time of day a reception is held. Finger foods and hors d'oeuvres will meet the appetite needs of guests and reduce the food cost per person. Often a coordinator will know food vendors from another setting with whom they can negotiate for a reasonable price.

Creative bargaining and borrowing are vital to saving money while still creating an elegant reception. Most caterers are not locked into package meals, if they think they can make a sale. Dropping the most expensive menu items—which most guests will not like anyway—can save substantial dollars.[2]

Unless a couple is committed to linen, china, and silver, another huge savings usually comes in avoiding rental of linens, silverware and dishes. For example, you can purchase three very high quality (almost indistinguishable from cloth) paper table covers for the rental price of one linen tablecloth. If renting is the only option, then the coordinator should rent for the family, rather than the caterer—who usually marks up the cost with a service fee.

BORROW, BORROW, BORROW

It's amazing how many people keep part or all of their wedding decorations. And they are glad to see them used again, in a new setting. By borrowing from several families, a creative friend can reassemble pieces into an entirely new, and beautiful arrangement. Again, simplicity is the key for beautiful design.

---

2 In our setting, we were able to create our own package and reduce the cost by one-half.

SPEND A LITTLE EXTRA TO GO GREEN

No longer is it acceptable, especially for Jesus-followers, to continue destroying creation by the use of plastic and Styrofoam.

There is no question.

We now know the damage we are causing to God's world that we were commanded to care for, and we must act differently.

Going green is quite easy and makes a statement about your ministry and it's concern for all humanity.[3] And although the cost is somewhat greater than the regular polluting products, it is not prohibitive—and worth it.

So, if a couple is planning to use disposable supplies, they can search out the many on-line suppliers of 100% compostable and 100% biodegradable options.[4] Vendors now offer crystal clear beverage cups and table service made out of PLA (vegetable starch), paper plates made from bagasse (sugar-cane pulp), and coffee cups made from 100% recycled paper.

The primary reason for using 100% compostable and biodegradable products is that since they will soon return completely to the soil there is no need to separate the recyclables when cleaning up—everything goes into the trash. In a simple way we have the opportunity to make creation stewardship a reality.

Another option is to purchase quantities of stainless tableware, and dishes, from a discount or restaurant supply store. Then donate the items to a thrift store, another couple (who would share costs), or a homeless center, following the ceremony. The downside of reusable products is that someone must wash them.

ADDITIONAL THOUGHTS

If a family or couple shows no interest in following your guidance for escaping the excesses of weddings and receptions, nothing you say may make a difference to them.

---

3 Make sure to place notes in the wedding program and/or scatter small signs around the reception tables declaring your care for the world because you follow Jesus. A couple may also announce that they have simplified the wedding and reception, and will be contributing some of the money saved to a special not-for-profit ministry.

4 A good site: www.worldcentric.org.

You cannot dictate their behavior.

Yet don't give up. There will be couples whom you work with that will jump at the chance. They may or may not be Jesus-followers, but they know that there are bigger human and spiritual issues at stake than extravagant living.

You can then offer them the opportunity to make a difference in the world.

10

CLOSING THOUGHTS — CARING FOR THE FRAGILE PEOPLE

Why close with a chapter about fragile people in a book about weddings and marriage?

Good question! Simple answer!

They are the flip-side of the happy couple standing at the wedding altar. Fragile people are those most impacted when relationships are not healthy and marriages go bad.

And while each section that follows is presented as a topic, we must remember each topic represents humans who live with the struggles being discussed. Those issues we wish we could wave a magic wand over and watch each troubled relationship bounce back to full health. But as you know, no such wand exists.

While each topic deserves an individual book, hopefully this brief sample will raise your awareness to the issues and encourage further digging. You will need to nose around your own community to discover the issues that need your specific attention.

As ministry leaders we care about at-risk people. We want to serve those who are in pain or experiencing loss. We want to stand with the fragile people. Yet, in the rush of life and ministry, we can easily overlook those who most need us, unless we intentionally turn our focus toward them.

And just as in Jesus' day, there are multitudes of fragile people in, or near our faith communities.

CHILDREN OF COHABITATING COUPLES

One of the most neglected groups in our culture is children of cohabitating couples. Since so much has already been discussed about the dangers of cohabitation, we may need only add, "Watch out for the kids."

One of the greatest problems for children living with a cohabitating couple is the high probability the couple will break up. Fully three quarters of children born to cohabitating parents will see their parents split up before they reach age sixteen, whereas only about a third of children born to married parents face a similar fate.

Parental break up...almost always entails a myriad of personal and social difficulties for children.... Several studies have found that children currently living with a mother and her unmarried partner have significantly more behavior problems and lower academic performance than children in intact families.[1]

CHILDREN OF DIVORCE

The data concerning the issues suffered by children of divorced parents can be contradictory, depending on what point the researcher wants to make.

However, there are several factors to keep in mind.

⇨ Children whose parents divorce need special care from the faith community. In order for children to learn permanence in relationships, they need models that their parents don't provide. They also need to sense that they are valued and not the reason for their parents' unhappiness. The faith community can provide such a supportive place.

⇨ It is a popular lie that insists children of divorced parents are better off than children who live in families with parental conflict.

A recent large-scale, long-term study suggests...[that]...while parents' marital unhappiness and discord have a broad negative impact on

1 "Should We Live Together?" Popenoe and Whitehead, 8.

virtually every dimension of their children's wellbeing, so does the fact of going through a divorce.... It was only the children in **very high-conflict**[2] homes who benefited from the conflict removal that divorce may bring. In **lower-conflict** marriages that end in divorce—and the study found that perhaps as many as two-thirds of the divorces were of this type—the situation of the children was made much worse following a divorce.... Therefore, except in the minority of high-conflict marriages it is better for the children if their parents stay together and work out their problems than to divorce.[3]

If you are able to provide care for divorced persons, offer care for their kids as well.

⇨ Children, especially girls, of divorced parents (and cohabiting couples) are highly vulnerable to sexual abuse. There's not space to warn of the many dangers to girls from predators—sometimes the stepfather or stepbrother—who prey upon girls whose parents divorce.[4]

Be alert for signs of abuse. You must intervene—never ignore them.

DEVALUED PARENTS

Devalued parenthood is a quickly growing issue; an issue we must no longer avoid in a healthy faith community.

It was during the last third of the 20th century that having children stopped being an indispensable element of couplehood and became a marriage option. Certainly, increased birth-control methods and concern for the burgeoning world population were important factors.

Yet with the changing attitudes toward children have come a devaluing of couples who take on the adventure of parenting. While we may argue the many reasons for the shift, the shift is a reality.

"The presence of children in America has declined significantly since 1960, as measured by fertility rates and the percentage of house-

---

2   **Bold** emphasis, the author's.

3   "The Top Ten Myths of Divorce," by David Popenoe, The National Marriage Project, Rutgers, The State University of New Jersey (March 2004), p. 2. Document available at http://marriage.rutgers.edu/publications/pubtoptenmyths.htm.

4   See "Fractured families, fragile children—the sexual vulnerability of girls in the aftermath of divorce," by Robin Fretwell Wilson, *Children and Family Law Quarterly,* Vol. 14, No. 1, 2002.

holds with children. Other indicators suggest that this decline has reduced the child centeredness of our nation and contributed to the weakening of the institution of marriage."[5]

In previous generations, teens usually moved into young adult life with its marriage responsibilities and child rearing. As couples aged toward the releasing time of their children they also faced retirement and death soon followed. Life insurance policies and retirement plans that kick in at age 65 anticipate this typical lifecycle.

But now most USAmericans are living longer and many have the income to retire early. Thus, parenting no longer takes up the major portion of a couple's life, nor is it the heart of their life mission. It is often something to simply endure.

Advertisers have taken full advantage of this cultural shift. We are urged to continue acting and purchasing like teenagers into our 30s and 40s—extending adolescence well beyond the teen years. So instead of helping our teens become young adults we attempt to keep our young adults living as teens.

And since we seniors, on the other end of life's spectrum, are living longer, we seduce ourselves into reverting back to adolescence as soon as we can find the time and financial means. Golf and erectile dysfunction treatments are the toys of choice. The result is the collapsing of the parenting years into a smaller and smaller slice of life, and parents feeling left out of the excitement if they choose to invest in their kids.

Parents need our affirmation, encouragement, and attention. And since both spouses usually work outside the home to pay the bills, most children end up at some point in a day care. We've done it. However, resourcing and supporting parents—even to the point of creating the highest quality parent-involved daycare—can make a world of difference in helping them to be the very best in their parenting ministry.

EARLY PUBESCENT CHILDREN

Early pubescence has enormous ramifications for our children. Research documented four primary causes (stress, childhood obesity, father-absence, and television—including video/computer watching) for why our children are hitting puberty earlier and earlier. And with the com-

---

5 "The State of Our Unions 2007: The Social Health of Marriage in America," p. 21.

ing of early pubescence (as early as 7 year old) comes the crisis of sexual ripening in a culture permeated with sexuality. The result is probable sexual involvement without the moral or emotional maturity to understand what is transpiring. Thus we have children having babies.

Our children are facing adult issues and parenting long before arriving at adulthood.

Let's take a quick look at these four key issues.

Stress—Our children face stresses from multiple fronts, simultaneously. These crises include:
- parental separation
- over-achieving parents seeking to involve their kids in every status-climbing program or sports program available
- pressure for academic achievement
- exposure to crisis news broadcasts, describing an uncertain world
- too much high-stimulus media viewing
- economic struggles
- changing family relationships and family structures

And the list could go on.

Early Childhood Obesity—Since childhood obesity has gained high visibility in many venues we can limit discussion here. Suffice it to say, the care of our children's health involves more than just eating and exercise. It impacts the entire set of childhood health systems.

Due partly to efforts of people like Michelle Obama (wife of President Barack Obama), the latest reports of decreasing obesity among children are encouraging.

Father Absence—We are finally recognizing the huge impact father-absence places on children. This does not reduce the significant impact of mothers. Mothers are the usually the nurturing centers of families. And most single-parent families are led by mothers.

As research has now focused on the impact to children, especially daughters, without a dad, some surprising information is surfacing.

We know that the pheromones given off by a biological father delay the onset of puberty in a daughter.

We also know that the pheromones given off by a non-biological male in the home can cause early pubescence in a daughter; the result when new husbands, boyfriends or step-brothers are living with a mom and her daughters.

One dramatic study shows that…

> *Overall, "the quality of fathers' investment in the family emerged as the most important feature of the proximal family environment relative to daughters' pubertal timing." Regarding the data's implications, the authors stress the connection between a father's absence and some of the most serious social problems facing adolescent girls: "early pubertal maturation, risky sexual behavior and early age of first birth are all components of an integrated reproductive strategy that derives, in part, from low paternal investment."*[6]

So, in a faith-community, where a culture of healthy relationships is valued, we will help moms protect their father-absent daughters; to be those surrogate parents who stand alongside.

Television And Video/Computer Viewing—Before you write me off, listen to what is being discovered about the impact of light on the pineal gland.

First, the pineal gland, a tiny gland at the base of the brain, produces melatonin. Melatonin impacts the body's developmental clock. Throughout childhood, high levels of melatonin are produced. Melatonin levels begin declining at the onset of puberty.

---

6 "Propositions" by David Blankenhorn, *USA Today*, May 8, 2001. "Propositions" is a periodic research summary from the Institute for American Values, 1841 Broadway, Suite 211, New York, NY 10023; see also info@americanvalues.org. Other sources to extend your research:
  a. "Father-Daughter Relationships Crucial to When Girls Enter Puberty…" a research summary from Vanderbilt University found in *Science Daily* at <http://www.sciencedaily.com/releases/1999/09/990927064822.htm>.
  b. "The Young Black Women" by Reginald J. Eadie, a research article found at <http://eatandlivelonger.com/youngbw.html>.
  c. "Father Absence and Early Family Composition as a Predictor of Menarcheal Onset: Psychosocial and Familial Factors that Mitigate Pubertal Timing" by Amanda Healey; a Master of Arts thesis at East Tennessee State University, 2006.

While research continues, artificial light seems to highly impact the production of melatonin by the pineal gland. Thus, long hours of artificial light cause the reduction of melatonin by the pineal gland, which sets off puberty at earlier ages.

The mechanism behind melatonin production is poorly understood. But it is thought that prolonged exposure to artificial light reduces the body's production of melatonin, whereas experiencing regular intervals of natural sunlight and darkness increases it....

"US studies have shown that the greater the exposure to television, the earlier the age of sexual experience, including teenage pregnancies."[7]

In addition, there are studies that show the impact of television (meaning anything with a lighted video screen) on many other health issues including obesity, heart trouble, eyesight, autism, attention span, brain growth, IQ, etc. Certainly we cannot turn back the decades to where people got up at sunrise and went to bed at dark. It would be more healthy but not possible in our world.

What's an alternative?

How might we coach families in rearing their children, in a culture that quickly farms their kids out to digital babysitting?

How might we help families learn to spend time together, turning off the artificial light sources more frequently, and grow deeper and healthier as a family? That's something to discuss when you gather with your discipleship team or your governing board.

BLENDED FAMILIES

As mentioned earlier, maybe the most fragile relationships in your faith-community are the blended families. Much is written showing the treacherous issues of blending two families, but usually too little action is taken to help them survive.

For the children, kids are generally no better off in a blended fam-

---

7 "Television Watching May Hasten Puberty," by Gaia Vince, June 28, 2004 at <www.newscientist.com>. Other research summaries can be found at <www.wellness.com> and www.aacap. org/cs/root/facts_for_families/children_and_watching_tv (American Academy of Child and Adolescent Psychiatry). While the internet is NOT the best source for reliable research, it is a beginning point.

ily than in a single parent family. While that may seem startling, when you think about the issues of blending two families, it's not so hard to envision the difficulties that the family members may experience.

More than other couples you perform weddings for, re-marrying couples need to work through the marriage preparation process with special care.[8] Usually they will need additional counseling. Too often people coming from previous marriages believe they've figured out what went wrong with their previous relationship, so they don't need to "waste the time" in premarital coaching. The truth is, they are the most needy. I would recommend that previously married couples (even if they are widowed and not divorced) start with FOCCUS, then proceed to meet with a Mentor Couple. The Mentor Couple should follow-up with REFOCCUS or a similar tool, about six months after the wedding.

SEXY, LONELY SENIORS

When I think of fragile people my mind is not naturally drawn toward sexually promiscuous senior citizens. But recent reports have forced me to reconsider.

The evidence is still coming as to whether the dramatic increase in AIDS and other STDs [sexually transmitted diseases] among senior adults is strictly a Florida phenomenon or a national epidemic. In the spring of 2006, reports began to surface of STD outbreaks in Florida retirement communities. On May 27, 2006, Channel 6, WKMG in Orlando, reported on Florida's largest retirement community in an article entitled "STDs Running Rampant in Retirement Community." Since then, several research projects have followed.[9]

While the hard data is sketchy, three Florida counties report 13%-15% of all AIDS cases are among retirees. The anecdotal evidence is even more compelling as stories emerge of black market Viagra, sexual activity in golf carts, and one-night stands among the males who take advantage of a 10:1 ratio between females and males. In one commu-

---

8 This is true for divorced persons, those who have cohabitated, or those whose spouse is deceased. All face similar issues of attempting to merge their relational past into the new one.

9 As an example see "AIDS: A growing problem for seniors" by Mona Gallagher reported on www.helium.com/items/226670-aids-a-growing-problem. Where research has begun in retirement communities outside Florida, similar results are surfacing.

nity a senior said the key question among friends was "Should I bring the little blue pill over tonight?"

Easy access to erectile dysfunction medications, no risk of pregnancy, earlier (and healthier) retiring males, lack of sex education, and loneliness are the most frequently mentioned causes for this growing promiscuity. Whatever the cause, the issue is one we cannot ignore.

Some of us will respond to the emerging data by assuming Christian communities are immune to improper sexual activity. Maybe true but probably not. Even if it is true, we are not excused from our mission to the world. Our mission calls us to the larger human community who strive for life meaning in a sex-charged, pleasure-driven culture. Retirement without purpose can only go so far toward fulfillment.

As I ponder the aging of our baby-boomer generation, a vision is beginning to emerge. Imagine an older generation who commit themselves to radically follow Jesus. Imagine releasing thousands of persons from retirement into a new ministry career. Imagine younger generations nurtured by seniors' experience and wisdom. Yes, the needs are immense; the opportunities even greater.

AND THAT'S NOT ALL!

While the paragraphs above describe some at-risk persons, it's obvious that the list is incomplete. Your mind has probably flashed around your neighborhood or faith-community and recalled many similar, yet different, difficult situations.

I've not intended this discussion to frighten you. Instead, I hope by listing a few of the obvious situations, you'll live more alertly, lead more intentionally—and passionately guide your people into a healthy community where everyone watches out for everyone else.

Our era of pain and hopelessness is probably no worse than previous generations, but is certainly more public. Yet, we have an opportunity to provide a sharp contrast, to live as hope-filled, healthy people who walk alongside those in pain.

We can cast a vision of God's possibilities.

We can pass on the hope.

We can, as Sam Shoemaker said years ago, point others "inside the door" ... the door we too have found.[10]

> If God is really God;
>   if Jesus truly lived, died, and resurrected;
> and if the Holy Spirit is still active in the world,
> Then God's restoration power,
>   from brokenness to reconciliation,
> from unhealth to full-health,
> is possible for any relationship.
> Count on it!
> Live in it!
> Lead like it!

---

10 See "I Stay Near the Door—An Apologia For My Life," a poem by The Reverend Canon Samuel M. Shoemaker, Jr, Episcopal priest, instrumental in the Oxford Group and the founding of Alcoholics Anonymous. This poem was published at Calvary Rectory, Pittsburgh, PA, Christmas, 1958. (The poem can be found at: http://mauihistorian.blogspot.com/2012/10/aas-rev-shoemaker-so-i-stay-near-door.html.)

APPENDIX

Go Ahead, Copy It... But

On the following pages you'll find samples of many of the materials we've used in marriage ministry.

Plagiarism is never right—but there is no need to reinvent the wheel, unless you have specific need for a new wheel. In other words, feel free to start with the samples we've created, then adapt, edit, or rewrite to fit your ministry needs and context.

But giving credit for others' contribution to your ministry shows your people that
- You're willing to cooperate with others to create a better ministry AND
- You're willing to show gratitude for those contributions.

So, someplace on every document you create from our samples, PLEASE ADD the following citation:

(Feel free to use a really small font, such as Times New Roman or Arial at 7–8 points)

"Adapted by permission. © 2015 by Daryl L. Smith.
Additional resources and information at www.DonQDox.org."

SAMPLE RESOURCES:

DOCUMENT 1—WEDDING INFORMATION PACKET

[Print on the envelope that will hold all materials that you want couples to read before the approval appointment.]

Wedding Information Packet

Are you planning a wedding at <Your Church Name>?
Please read the enclosed information first.

When you're ready for an approval interview with a pastor, please complete the Wedding Interview Information Form, return it to the church office and we'll set an appointment for you. We're here to help!

DOCUMENT 2—WEDDING INTERVIEW
INFORMATION FORM

[You may want to use an 8½ x 11 page, folded in half]

Wedding Interview Form

Proposed wedding time _____
Proposed Location _____
Rehearsal date/time _____
Today's date _____

Wedding Interview

BRIDE'S INFORMATION

Name _____
Address _____
City _____
State _____ Zip Code _____
Cell _____ Email _____
Birth date _____
Education Completed _____

Church Attending _____

Church Member? ☐ Y ☐ N

Married Previously? ☐ Y ☐ N Divorced? ☐ Y ☐ N Widowed? ☐ Y ☐ N

    Children? _____

    How many? _____

    Does the family approve the marriage? _____

GROOM'S INFORMATION

Name _____

Address _____

City _____

State _____ Zip Code _____

Cell _____ Email _____

Birth date _____

Education Completed _____

Church Attending _____

Church Member? ☐ Y ☐ N

Married Previously? ☐ Y ☐ N Divorced? ☐ Y ☐ N Widowed? ☐ Y ☐ N

    Children? _____

    How many? _____

    Does the family approve the marriage? _____

INIDIVIDUAL BACKGROUND

BRIDE

1. When did Jesus become more than a word to you, if he ever has? Please share a bit of your story:

    _____

    _____

    _____

    _____

2. What church experiences have you had?

    _____

    _____

    _____

    _____

3. Give a brief overview of your family background, parents, siblings, where you grew up, etc.:

    _____

    _____

    _____

    _____

GROOM

1. When did Jesus become more than a word to you, if he ever has? Please share a bit of your story:

    _____

    _____

    _____

    _____

2. What church experiences have you had?

    _____

    _____

    _____

    _____

3. Give a brief overview of your family background, parents, siblings, where you grew up, etc.:

    _____

    _____

    _____

    _____

AS A COUPLE

How long have you been going together? _____

How long have you been engaged? _____

Where do you plan to live after marriage? _____

Will you be attending our church? _____

Are you currently living together? _____

Have you attended any premarital counseling? _____

Have you attended Engaged Encounter? _____
What books about marriage have you read?

_____

_____

Can you name any couples in our church who know you well?

_____

If previously divorced.
(If both are previously divorced, please duplicate and respond separately.)

When were you divorced? _____
What circumstances led to the divorce?

_____

_____

_____

Is your former spouse remarried? _____
What steps have you taken toward reconciliation?

_____

If you have children, explain their attitude toward your remarriage.

_____

"Adapted by permission. © 2015 by Daryl L. Smith.
Additional resources and information at www.DonQDox.org."

DOCUMENT 3—GENERAL WEDDING INFORMATION

[Text for a brochure or web page.]

Weddings at <Your Church Name>

Congratulations on your engagement! This is a wonderful time of love, dreams, and plans—filled with joy and activity. As you anticipate your marriage and try to get all the wedding pieces into place, remember our goal is to walk with you. We are here, as your faith community, to help you celebrate a great wedding day and launch a committed, life-long marriage together.

<Church Name> celebrates Christian marriage.

We believe God established the sanctity of marriage and intends the bond to last a lifetime. In following those beliefs, <Church Name> has the responsibility to do everything possible to help every couple getting married at <Church Name> to achieve a permanent marriage bond and establish a strong Christian home.

<Church Name> is available for weddings of church members and regular attendees. All weddings are scheduled in the <office/department> under the supervision of a <Church Name> pastor.

Weddings performed in the church will follow the <Church Name> wedding guidelines.

Rental fees apply and are used to cover expenses incurred by the church. A schedule of fees is available from the church office.

When Planning Your Wedding
Please keep the following in mind.

1. One of the <Church Name> pastors is responsible to oversee and approve each wedding ceremony performed here. Visiting pastors and ordained ministers are welcome to assist.

2. Pre-marital counseling, with a <Church Name> pastor, completion of the pre-marital inventory, attendance at a minimum of six follow-up sessions with a Mentor Couple, and regular church attendance are prerequisites for all weddings held at <Church Name>. During the first year of marriage the Mentor Couple will administer a post-wedding inventory and conduct follow-up sessions. Engaged Encounter is highly recommended and may be required along with other specific requirements made by your officiating pastor.

3. A <Church Name> Wedding Coordinator is required to assist the pastor and the couple at each wedding. A list of Coordinators is provided after the Approval Interview with the <Church Name> pastor. The Wedding Coordinator will guide you through the many wedding details and act as the church contact person. They will guide the rehearsal and wedding so you and your families can focus on the wedding ceremony instead of the details.

To get started, your wedding should be put on the church calendar at least six months prior to the anticipated wedding date. Stop by the church office to obtain the Wedding Information Packet. Return the Wedding Interview Information Form to the church and ask to schedule an Approval Interview with a <Church Name> pastor.

Your wedding date will be tentatively reserved, if approved, and only finalized upon completion of the preparation requirements. A complete Wedding Handbook will be given to you after the Approval Interview.

Additional Notes

Completing all the details for a wedding (counseling, filling out forms, paying fees, etc.) may get frustrating but each is important, so all must be completed three months before the wedding.

Since we are committed to getting you started into a life-long and successful marriage, a <Church Name> pastor has the responsibility to delay or disapprove a wedding if he/she believes the wedding should not take place ... or until satisfactory completion of additional counseling.

Please read all information provided to you prior to the Approval Interview with the pastor. It is wise to evaluate your relationship in the context of the church's belief statements. Are there issues that you may need to work through before a wedding at <Church Name>?

If you have further questions, please call the church office. <insert all church contact information>

"Adapted by permission. © 2015 by Daryl L. Smith.
Additional resources and information at www.DonQDox.org."

DOCUMENT 4—THE MARRIAGE PREP CHECKLIST

Bride _____

Groom _____

Planned Wedding Date: _____

Preparation Start Date _____
(6 months prior to wedding date)

Please DATE EACH ITEM below as you complete it.

_____ Request a Wedding Information Packet
     Read all the materials
     Fill out the Wedding Interview Form
_____ Return the Wedding Interview Form and set the Initial
     Interview appointment with the pastor.
_____ Meet with the pastor for the Initial Interview.
_____ If wedding is approved, receive a Wedding Handbook.
_____ Select a Wedding Coordinator
     Set first appointment with Wedding Coordinator
_____ Return Wedding Reservation Form
_____ Pay Deposit
_____ Confirm that your wedding date is penciled in on
     the church calendar
_____ Select a Mentor Couple
     Schedule first session with Mentor Couple
_____ Complete the FOCCUS premarital inventory online.
     Pay processing fee
_____ Attend worship on a regular basis (as defined by pastoral staff)
     Dates in attendance: _____
_____ Complete a minimum of 6 sessions with the Mentor Couple
     Dates of sessions: _____
_____ HIGHLY RECOMMENDED: Attend Engaged Encounter

Check-In Date _____
(3 months prior to wedding date)

The Mentor Couple and the Pastor consult regarding your premarital inventory and sessions. A decision is made about your preparedness for marriage. Additional counseling or postponement may be recommended.

Final approval is given when all requirements have been met to the satisfaction of the Pastor and the Mentor Couple.

Ceremony Preparation _____
(3 months prior to wedding date)

_____ Begin meeting with Pastor to work on wedding ceremony.
_____ Receive books from Pastor

Pay all fees _____
(3 weeks prior to wedding date)
    Record of Payments:

    _____

    _____

WEDDING DAY (Congratulations!)

As Married Life Begins:
_____ Contact your Mentor Couple
_____ Set the first 9-month session with Mentor Couple
       to work on REFOCCUS
       Date: _____
_____ Complete REFOCCUS
_____ Meet with Mentor Couple
_____ Set one-year session with Mentor Couple
       Date: _____
_____ Meet with Mentor Couple for one-year "relationship checkup."
       The Mentor Couple and Pastor are available whenever you
       want or need to be in touch.

"Adapted by permission. © 2015 by Daryl L. Smith.
Additional resources and information at www.DonQDox.org."

DOCUMENT 5—MARRIAGE MINISTRY RESOURCES

[This is a small list of the BEST resources that are available.]

FOCCUS/REFOCUS

This is a great source for premarital and post-marital inventories/ materials. Contact FOCCUS, Inc., USA [Nazareth Hall, 3300 N. 60th St., Omaha, NE 68104-3402; 877.883.5422 or 402.827.3735]. Explore their website at www.FoccusInc.com. This group (and the materials they produce) is my favorite since they write from a Christian perspective, out of the Omaha Diocese (the creators of Marriage Encounter, decades ago).

Prepare/Enrich

Another great source for premarital and post-marital inventories is Prepare/Enrich (Life Innovations) [2660 Arthur St., Roseville, MN 55440; 800.331.1661]. Explore their website at www.prepareenrich. com. Many other resources are available on their website.

Les & Leslie Parrott

Les and Leslie Parrot may be the best at helping couples grow into healthy, life-long marriages. Check out their website—that is filled with materials, places they'll be speaking etc.—at www.LesandLeslie. com.

Retrouvaille

If you know couples whose marriage is in trouble but will take one more shot at recovery, this is the place to check. The sessions are led by people who have walked through the pain of brokenness and come out the other side. Information about programs in your area can be found at www.retrouvaille.org.

DOCUMENT 6—THE WEDDING COORDINATOR

[Text for information brochure or web page; you can also use this text to create a job description for your Wedding Coordinator.]

Here is how the WEDDING COORDINATOR will help you have a WONDERFUL WEDDING!

A <Your Church> Wedding Coordinator is required to assist the pastor and an engaged couple at each <Your Church> wedding. You will find their help to be invaluable.

Following approval of your wedding, you will contact a Wedding Coordinator from the list and set your first appointment date. The coordinator will review the church guidelines with you, help you fill out any forms, and answer your questions. They will also help to begin setting up the wedding. Coordinators work with you and the pastor to guide the rehearsal and the wedding so you and your family can focus on the wedding ceremony.

The following list describes the Wedding Coordinator's role in more detail. [You may want to make copies for your family members/ friends who are helping with the wedding.]

The Wedding Coordinator will:
- Meet with the bride and groom shortly after the wedding date is scheduled to begin the wedding planning process. [Both bride and groom are expected to be participants in the planning.]
  The Wedding Coordinator will NOT plan your wedding for you. She/he will check in periodically to make sure the details are covered.
  The Coordinator will review the entire wedding: entering, exiting, receiving line, receiving of gifts, people involved, etc.
- Make sure the couple has fulfilled all the pre-marital requirements (minimum of 3 months prior to the wedding).
- Meet with the bride and/or groom at least one month before the wedding to go over final information forms, to work out the

rehearsal schedule, to set a time-line for the wedding day, to final-
ize all wedding logistics (e.g. where people will stand).

- Guide the rehearsal with the pastor.
  Suggested rehearsal order:
    - o   Introduction of guests (the couple)
    - o   Prayer (pastor or coordinator)
    - o   Instructions for entering, leaving, standing, sound,
          lights, etc. (coordinator)
    - o   Wedding ceremony specifics (pastor)
    - o   Exiting process
    - o   Wedding day schedule for everyone
    - o   Instruction of ushers (coordinator)
- Manage details on the Wedding Day
    - o   Oversee the worship center set up and decorating.
    - o   Meet florist, photographer, videographer, etc., on their
          arrivals; go over final guidelines with each.
    - o   Oversee musicians, ushers, guest-book attendants, gift
          receivers, etc.
    - o   Get flowers to and on proper people. [Flowers are pinned
          on the way they grow—up, starting pin from outside
          through fabric, then stem, then fabric.]
    - o   Make sure that rings are in place.
    - o   Make sure that the Marriage License is present.
    - o   Make sure all candles are lit appropriately.
    - o   Make sure lighting and sound is cared for.
    - o   Guide everyone in and out of the wedding ceremony
          properly.
    - o   Set up receiving line.
    - o   Make sure the women's and men's dressing rooms are
          cleaned.

ADDITIONAL NOTES for a Wedding Coordinator:
1. The pastor and Wedding Coordinator will work closely together
   during the entire wedding planning in case there are problems that
   need to be resolved.
2. Remind the maid of honor to take the bride's flowers during the
   ceremony.

3. To arrange the bride's gown, lift and the air will allow it to fall into the correct place.

4. Remind the bride and groom to take a deep breath and look around before starting down the aisle. If they don't pause to notice what's happening, they won't remember most of the day.

5. Keep an ammonia capsule nearby—even with the pastor—in case someone starts to faint.

6. Most ring bearers and flower girls should sit with an adult. They are not usually able to stand in place during a ceremony.

7. Make sure air conditioning and heating equipment is set to keep the room comfortable.

"Adapted by permission. © 2015 by Daryl L. Smith.
Additional resources and information at www.DonQDox.org."

DOCUMENT 7—RECEPTION COORDINATOR

[Text for information brochure or web page; you can also use this text to create a job description for your Reception Coordinator.]

Here is how the RECEPTION COORDINATOR will guide you through an amazing RECEPTION!

A <Your Church> Reception Coordinator is required to guide any engaged couple who decides to hold their reception at <Your Church>.

Following approval of your wedding, and after acquiring your Wedding Coordinator, you will want to contact a Reception Coordinator from the list and set your first appointment date. The coordinator will review the church guidelines with you, and acquaint you with the facilities and equipment that are available to use. They will also help to begin setting up the reception.

[You may want to make copies of the following for your family members/friends who are helping with the reception.]

The Reception Coordinator will:
*   Meet with the bride and groom shortly after the wedding date is scheduled to help guide the reception planning.
    The Reception Coordinator will NOT plan your reception for you, but will work closely with you in the process.
*   Serve as the resource person for the bride and groom in planning the wedding reception, including the room decorating schedule. In some cases, the Reception Coordinator may recruit a team to decorate the reception hall. Thus, the family is not taking on that difficult task.
*   Meet with the bride and/or groom at least one month before the wedding to go over final form information and to set a time-line for the reception.
*   Coordinate room layout with the custodians.
*   Coordinate with the Wedding Coordinator in any areas that over-lap, making sure all forms are completed and all fees are paid.
*   Assist the bride and groom in recruiting helpers and knowing what jobs need to be cared for.

- Guide the ENTIRE Reception, making sure that:
  - o The caterer/food preparers have food ready on time.
  - o Food is in the proper locations.
  - o Flowers and other decorations are in the proper places.
  - o The cake is set up properly.
  - o Guests are greeted when they arrive.
  - o The reception is started on time.
  - o The MC is prepared with a script for introductions, etc.
  - o Bridal party is cared for.
  - o Musicians or DJs are prepared and perform appropriately.
  - o Lighting and sound is cared for.
  - o The schedule for cake-cutting, bouquet-throwing, etc., is followed.
  - o The bridal couple exits while there are still people to give a proper farewell.
  - o Clean-up crews complete their work correctly.

ADDITIONAL NOTES for the Reception Coordinator:

1. The Reception Coordinator and Wedding Coordinator will work closely together during the entire wedding planning in case there are problems that need to be resolved.
2. To get the cake cut appropriately,
   a. The bride should choose an experienced cake cutter, or one who can be taught.
   b. A second person is needed to help the cutter, hold the cake, work with the plates, etc.
   c. The knife should be at the cake table with a wet cloth for wiping after cutting.
   d. A second plate should be ready to receive the top layer of the cake.
   e. Servers should be on stand-by if cake is to be distributed to guests at their seats.
   f. Serving trays will be needed for each pair of servers, as one carries the cake and the other distributes.

DOCUMENT 8—SAMPLE WEDDING WORSHIP SCRIPT

[This outline is from the most comprehensive wedding I've performed. You will probably never include as much as we did in this worship. (Maybe the only piece we ommitted was a foot-washing ceremony for the bride and groom.) This wedding worship was held in the round with pastors usually in the middle. The bride and groom were brought to the middle of the worship center by their parents for giving to each other.]

PREPARATION
- Prelude

Music: _____
- Stage candles lit
- Candle lighting and seating of the GRANDPARENTS
  (center aisle to candle table, then on to front seats)

CREATION
- Processional

Music: _____
- Pastor moves from STAGE RIGHT to STAGE CENTER
- Bridesmaids & Groomsmen

(Couples enter from back doors, down Center Aisle to front, stage top)
- Ring bearer/Flower girl

[CONGREGATION STAND]
- Bride & Groom and Parents ENTRANCE

Music: _____
- Groom and parents (South Aisle)
- Bride and parents (North Aisle) [meet at center Candle Table]
- Call to Worship (Pastor)

   Dear friends, it is with great joy that we welcome you to this celebration of love. We gather in the sight of God and the presence of these witnesses for an awesome and sacred event; the joining together of <GROOM> and <BRIDE> in marriage.

   Please honor the sacred nature of these moments by turning off your pagers, cell phones and flash cameras until the close of the ceremony.

Marriage is a treasured and honored, life-long relationship, given to us from the hand of our gracious God at the time of creation. Since then it has been safeguarded by the laws of Moses; affirmed in scripture by the words of the prophets; and blessed by the teaching and example of our Lord and Savior Jesus Christ.

So it is, we have been invited here today not just to observe a sacred ceremony. We are gathered as followers of Jesus for a wedding worship—a time for us to enter with our hearts into every song, every prayer, every scripture—yes, every sacred moment. And for those of us who are married, let this be a recommitment of our vows to our spouses.

May we each encounter the amazing love of God, as we reflect on Creation, remember the New Covenant in Christ, join in Commissioning <BRIDE> and <GROOM> for ministry, and then meet for a great Celebration reception.
[SEAT CONGREGATION]

• Giving of the Bride and Groom (Pastor)
[To the Bride's Parents:]
   <FATHER & MOTHER>, do you give <BRIDE> to <GROOM>, and promise to support their new union with your love? If so, please respond with "we do."
[Parents respond]

[To the Groom's Parents]
   <FATHER & MOTHER>, do you give <GROOM> to <BRIDE>, and promise to support their new union with your love? If so please respond with "we do."
[Parents respond]
[To the congregation]
   Now to rest of us, as <BRIDE> and <GROOM>s friends and family, will you promise to support their new union with your love, holding them accountable to the vows they will make today? If so please respond: "With God's help we will."
[Congregation responds]

• Lighting of Family Candles
[MOTHERS light family candles]
• Invocation (Pastor) *[INSERT TEXT]*
[Parents seated]
[Groom and Bride move to floor at base of CENTER steps]
• Scripture #1: Genesis 1:27; 2:4–8a, 15, 18–24 *[INSERT TEXT]*
READER(S):_____
• Declaration of Intent (Pastor)

To affirm the purpose for our gathering with you today,
<GROOM> and <BRIDE>, let me ask each of you to share your
intentions here before God and these witnesses:

<GROOM>, will you have <BRIDE> to be your wife,…
<BRIDE>, will you have <GROOM> to be your husband,…
• Pouring of the Sand (Pastor)

<BRIDE> and <GROOM>, you, along with all humanity,
originated through the amazing, imaginative power of God, molding
the sand of this earth. God then took those first humans, poured his
likeness into them, breathing into them the breath of God. And God
declared them exceedingly good.

In that fertile garden, the first woman and first man walked to-
gether with God, basking in God's creation dream for every man and
every woman. The dream of knowing an unimagined oneness—joined
in partnership for the journey of life—and a life of worship with their
Creator.

As you pour together your individual vials of sand with mine,
(symbolizing God your Creator), note that the individual colors
remain, while mixed together—as will your lives, as a man and
woman in relation to God. May this mixed sand represent your lives so
that you experience the oneness of God's dream and are so focused on
Christ, that God will declare your marriage partnership exceedingly
good.

[GROOM, BRIDE and PASTOR move UP STEPS to pour sand]
• Congregational Song: _____
Leader: _____
[ATTENDANTS MOVE TO SIDE]
[GROOM, BRIDE, PASTOR POUR SAND]

[GROOM and BRIDE RETURN to front of stage, facing congregation.]

[ATTENDANTS MOVE TO PLACE]

[PASTOR moves to floor in front of stage.]

COVENANT

• Scripture #2: Philippians 2:1–11 *[INSERT TEXT]*

READER(S):_____

• Homily (Pastor)

CREATION...

The FIRST Scripture reading in Genesis propelled our minds from this room, back to that very first wedding.

That day when the Holy Trinity said, "Let's climax this creation by making humans—beings into whom we can pour our very own image. And, let's create them to enjoy the deep, amazing relationship—the ONENESS—that we enjoy."...[INSERT TEXT]

COVENANT...

Finally and fortunately, however, Jesus arrived on the scene as God's love in human skin; inviting us to come home to our Creator. To teach us how to live and love as God lives and loves....[INSERT TEXT]

COMMISSION...

<GROOM> and <BRIDE>, you know that you are called to share that Good News. Your lives have already touched countless lives. And your ministry will be expanded as you minister together....[INSERT TEXT]

CELEBRATION...

As your parents, family and friends, we are grateful that we have this opportunity to celebrate today with you. But more importantly, we look forward to celebrating the life-long marriage you begin today, partnering together in ministry, and totally given to Jesus—a life of celebrative worship. We can hardly wait to see what God does in and through you—as you walk this journey in God's Spirit....[INSERT TEXT]

• Vows (Pastor)

<GROOM> and <BRIDE>, you will now declare your love and commitment to one another with vows before these witnesses and God.

Please repeat after me.
GROOM RECITES:

<BRIDE>, I thank God for you, and choose you to be my wife. I promise to be faithful to you forever, to love and serve you as Christ served us. In joy and sorrow, sickness and health, for richer or poorer, and for all else this life may bring, I will be there to comfort and support you, encouraging you in all that God has created you to be. I take you <BRIDE> as my wife and best friend until death do us part.
BRIDE RECITES:

<GROOM>, I thank God for you, and choose you to be my husband. I promise to be faithful to you forever, to love and serve you as Christ served us. In joy and sorrow, sickness and health, for richer or poorer, and for all else this life may bring, I will be there to comfort and support you, encouraging you in all that God has created you to be. I take you <GROOM> as my husband and best friend until death do us part.

• Exchange of Rings (Pastor) *[INSERT TEXT]*
• The Pronouncement (Pastor)

<BRIDE> and <GROOM>, by the authority given to me as a minister of Jesus Christ, I do declare that you, <GROOM> and <BRIDE>, are now husband and wife, according to the ordinances of God and the laws of this state, in the name of the Father, the Son, and the Holy Spirit. What God has joined together, let no one separate. YOU MAY NOW CELEBRATE YOUR MARRIAGE WITH A KISS!

• Solo: _____
SOLOIST: _____
[ATTENDANTS move to chairs]
[Pastor moves to Communion Table]
[GROOM and BRIDE move to STAGE LEFT]
• Scripture #3: Romans 8:35, 37, 38–39 *[INSERT TEXT]*
[Congregation in unison, PASTOR lead]

• Holy Communion (Pastor)

Friends, as <GROOM> and <BRIDE> begin their new life together, they invite you to join with them in the remembrance of Jesus the Christ and His sacrifice for us...[INSERT TEXT]

The invitation to partake of the bread and the cup is to all of us. This is not a denominational table. It's the table of Jesus—the place to remember that it is only through his death on the cross that the New Covenant between God and humans became available. We are now able to come home to our Creator and to experience life in all its abundance.

Jesus simply asks those who would join Him in this feast to be willing to respond to his love by giving ourselves back to him so he can continue making us into the persons we were created to be.

In the night of his betrayal, Jesus took bread, broke it and gave it to his disciples...

In a similar way, Jesus took the cup, blessed it...

Let's pray: [INSERT TEXT]

_____

Just a brief word of instruction: We will have <FOUR> stations of bread and juice, around the room.

You may come to partake when you're ready—at whatever station is closest or available. We will take by intinction—your server will break off a piece of bread for you, then you may dip the corner into the juice and eat it.

Servers, please come forward. [HAND WASH]

[Pastor partakes then serves SERVERS]

[Servers go to stations]

TO CONGREGATION: *Let us partake with thanksgiving!*

[GROOM and BRIDE kneel on KNEELER]

• Pastor serves BRIDE and GROOM

• Pastor serves attendants

• Attendants move to license-signing table

• Marriage License signing

• Signed by Pastor

• Co-signers: Maid of Honor and Best Man

• Keepsake Certificate signed by all attendants

[Check on Communion serving]

• CLOSE HOLY COMMUNION WITH PRAYER: *[INSERT TEXT]*

[BRIDE, GROOM, PASTOR move to Family-Candle TABLE]

COMMISSION

- Scripture #4: Matthew 5:14–16 *[INSERT TEXT]*
READER(S):_____

- Unity Candle (Pastor)

<BRIDE> and <GROOM>, as we began this ceremony, grand-parent candles were lit and parent family candles were lit, and there are roses on the table to represent those grandparents not with us today—all to symbolize your families of origin—those deep heritages that you bring together. In a moment you will take your family candles and light the Unity Candle, signifying your oneness with Christ and with each other.

By lighting this candle you publicly proclaim your intention for your marriage to shine brightly for Christ in ways brighter and clearer than you ever could alone.

You have also chosen to leave your family candles burning as a reminder that you will continue to honor and value the role your families have played and will continue to play as a source of love and encouragement in the years to come....[INSERT TEXT]

[GROOM and BRIDE light Unity Candle]

- Candle Lighting Ceremony (Pastor)

God has brought you two together, not only for one another but for the world. You are called to ministry both individually and as a couple. We now join as a congregation in Commissioning you for whatever God has in mind for you and wherever he leads. You have amazing gifts and God has great plans.

As a symbol of the mission that God has called you to, each of us holds a candle. We ask you to light a candle from your Unity Candle, and begin passing the flame to each of us. As the flame spreads across this congregation, may the presence of Christ in you, and in your mar-riage, spread across this world to bring transformation through God's love to multitudes of people.

A word of instruction: As the flame is brought to you, please dip your candle into the flame, keeping the flame upright.

[GROOM and BRIDE turn with lighted candles, lighting the first candle on each row, down the center aisle. Ushers will be ready with candles to help move flame across the aisles.

MUSIC: _____

By: _____

[Pastor takes lighted candle to the stage, lighting the attendant's candles.]

[ATTENDANTS STAND to light candles and REMAIN STANDING]

[BRIDE and GROOM return to KNEELER]

• Prayer of Commission and Blessing (Pastor) [INSERT TEXT]

NOTE TO THE CONGREGATION: *While <BRIDE> and <GROOM>'s mission together is just beginning, for safety sake, we must EXTINGUISH OUR CANDLES. But remember, just as <GROOM> and <BRIDE> have symbolized their mission through the light of these candles, as followers of Jesus we also carry the flame of his light in our hearts, to those who need the hope of Jesus.*

CELEBRATION

ANNOUNCEMENT: (Pastor)

Friends, our worship will not end in this room. Our lives aren't separated into sections of sacred and secular. Instead, we are called to total lives of worship before God. In a moment we will close this part of the ceremony and move into another form of worship—that of CELEBRATION.

We will join together in the <RECEPTION HALL> to eat, to listen to music, to dance, to play games, to converse, to reminisce—all in great joy for the marriage of <GROOM> and <BRIDE>—and in gratitude for what God has begun and blessed in this room.

Let me give you a brief word concerning the reception schedule.

[INSERT NEEDED TEXT]

• Benediction (Pastor) [INSERT TEXT]

• Introduction of Couple (Pastor) [INSERT TEXT]

• Recessional

• Dismissal of Congregation

[GROOM and BRIDE re-enter, dismiss rows, starting at the FRONT]

"Adapted by permission. © 2015 by Daryl L. Smith.
Additional resources and information at www.DonQDox.org."

DOCUMENT 9—PHOTOGRAPHER/VIDEOGRAPHER GUIDELINES

[Text for web page or information sheet. This works well as an 8½ x 11, front/back, cut in half; or as a folded card with the inside blank for notes.]

Photography/Videography for Weddings at <Your Church>

The photographer's/videographer's job is to record memories of the wedding day—especially the wedding worship ceremony.

However, he or she must never detract from the worship time.

Good photographers/videographers are rarely noticed as they work.

Therefore, the following guidelines are offered to assist you in doing your best work within the context of a wedding worship event.

SOME GUIDELINES...

- Photographer/videographers are always answerable to the direction of the <Your Church> pastor and the Wedding Coordinator. The Wedding Coordinator will give final instructions upon your arrival on the wedding day.
- If you are unfamiliar with the facility, you should visit before the wedding, to get a sense of location and lighting conditions.
- No photographs requiring special lighting or flash will be taken during the wedding ceremony—except as the bridal party processes and recesses. At that time you may shoot from halfway down the aisle from the back.
- The wedding coordinator will clarify any location directions that may not be clear to you.
- Please dress appropriately for the wedding. (If you are unsure about what is appropriate, check with the Wedding Coordinator.)
- Video cameras may be set, with guidance from the Wedding Coordinator, in the front of the worship center, as long as they are not obtrusvie and there is no movement during the wedding worship.
- No lights may be used during the worship for video shooting.

- It is best to leave the cameras running and unattended during the wedding worship.
- If a person must stay with the video camera, the person must get in place before the processional and not move until after the recessional.

NOTES:

"Adapted by permission. © 2015 by Daryl L. Smith.
Additional resources and information at www.DonQDox.org."

DOCUMENT 10—USHER GUIDELINES

[Text for web page or information sheet. This works well as an 8½ x 11, front/back, cut in half; or as a folded card with the inside blank for notes.]

Ushering for a Wedding at <Your Church>

Ushering is an amazing opportunity for service. You have the chance to help set the atmosphere for every guest who comes to the wedding worship celebration. Your attitude and spirit can make all the difference in how welcome the guests feel and how enthusiastically they participate in the celebration.

Meet with the Wedding Coordinator
- Unless told otherwise, you will meet in the lobby for instructions 45 minutes prior to the wedding. The Coordinator will give final directions at that time.

Personal Appearance
- Your clothing (usually formal) will be guided by the bride's and groom's preferences.
- Leave the gum at home, though a breath mint is good.
- Stand relaxed with hands at your side.

Seating of Guests
- Step toward the guests and ask, "May I help you find a seat?" Don't make them ask for help.
- If the center aisle is reserved for the wedding party, you will usher people down the outside aisles. Ask persons to move toward the center, to leave additional spaces for later arrivers.
- Usually, you will offer your arm to the first woman of the group. The men (and other women) will follow.
- Unless a man obviously needs assistance, you would not usually offer your arm to the man. He will follow.
- Facing the front, offer the arm on the same side of the aisle you will be seating the guests. For example, if seating on the left side, offer your left arm. When you reach the correct row, pivot back

away from the seats while releasing the woman's arm. This gives room for the guests to enter and specific direction for the row they are to use.

- Hand out programs—one to a couple or single as they are moving into their seats.
- Remind camera-carrying guests that NO FLASH may be used during the wedding worship ceremony.
- Attempt to seat the guest evenly on both sides of the worship center.
- At the planned wedding-start time, close the worship center doors. Latecomers may be seated in the rear of the worship center between sections of the worship—NEVER during a section.

Seating the Family

- According to the Wedding Coordinator's direction, immediate family members are usually ushered down the center aisle to the first or second row. Others are seated behind.
- Following the bridal party's recessional, the assigned ushers will usher parents and grandparents out of the worship center.
- If ushers are dismissing guests, you will release them row by row from the front of the worship center. The Wedding Coordinator will direct you.

NOTES:

"Adapted by permission. © 2015 by Daryl L. Smith. Additional resources and information at www.DonQDox.org."

DOCUMENT 11: WEDDING/RECEPTION HANDBOOK OUTLINE

[As you create your wedding material, you may want a wedding handbook/notebook to give to couples who have met approval requirements for a ceremony in your faith community. Here is a sample outline of the items that you can include. Add, delete, and fill in content that is appropriate for your ministry.]

THE WEDDING

I.   Overview

God created marriage to be a bond between a man and a woman that lasts a lifetime. At <Your Church> we take seriously our responsibility to help every couple achieve a permanent marriage bond and establish a strong Christian home. You may at times feel overwhelmed by forms and procedures, but we believe that each part of this marriage preparation process is significant.

Please feel free to talk with your Pastor, Wedding Coordinator, and Mentor Couple about any of your questions or any part of the process.

One key to planning a wedding at <Your Church> is this Wedding Handbook. It includes:

- Most of what you'll need to know about planning a wedding at <Your Church>. Please read it carefully.
- Various FORMS that you will need to complete and return.
- Information about planning a reception at <Your Church>.
- Places for you to keep handouts presented by your Pastor, Mentor Couple, Wedding Coordinator, and Reception Coordinator.

II. Steps to Securing a Wedding Date

III. Your Pastor
   a.   Initial Interview
   b.   Planning the wedding worship service
   c.   Counseling

IV. Your Mentor Couple and Marriage Counseling
   a.   Setting appointments
   b.   Meeting for a minimum of six sessions
   c.   Attending Engaged Encounter

V. Your Wedding Coordinator
   a.   Setting initial appointment
   b.   Job description and responsibilities

VI. Your Reception Coordinator
   a.   Setting initial appointment
   b.   Job description and responsibilities

VII. Facilities Available at <Your Church>
   a.   General policies for room usage
   b.   Worship Center
   c.   Fellowship Hall
   d.   Parlor and Conference Room
   e.   Nurseries
      i.   Policy for child care
      ii. Recruiting workers
   f.   Dressing Rooms
   g.   Arranging the stage and lobby areas, etc.

VIII. Other Important Guidelines
   a.   Days that weddings can be performed
   b.   Hours that facility is available
   c.   Holiday weekend weddings
   d.   Use of alcoholic beverages
   e.   Smoking policy

XVI. Important Guidelines
  a.   Available facilities
        i. Which rooms are usable for which size groups
        ii. Equipment usable in each room
  b.   Recruiting set-up and clean-up teams
  c.   Decorating time
  d.   Concluding time
  e.   Use of alcoholic beverages
  f.   Policy on smoking
  g.   Types and places for dancing
  h.   Kitchen and refrigerator use

XVII. Available Equipment
  a.   Dishes and tableware
  b.   Paper products
  c.   Tables and chairs
  d.   Linens
  e.   Silk Trees, etc.

XVIII. A Clean-up Checklist

"Adapted by permission. © 2015 by Daryl L. Smith.
Additional resources and information at www.DonQDox.org."

www.ingramcontent.com/pod-product-compliance
Lightning Source LLC
Chambersburg PA
CBHW071856020426
42331CB00010B/2546